REVISING YOUR DISSERTATION

REVISING YOUR DISSERTATION

ADVICE FROM LEADING EDITORS

UPDATED EDITION

With a New Foreword
by Sandford G. Thatcher

EDITED BY BETH LUEY

UNIVERSITY OF CALIFORNIA PRESS

Berkeley   Los Angeles   London

University of California Press, one of the most distinguished
university presses in the United States, enriches lives around the
world by advancing scholarship in the humanities, social sciences,
and natural sciences. Its activities are supported by the UC Press
Foundation and by philanthropic contributions from individuals
and institutions. For more information, visit www.ucpress.edu.

University of California Press
Berkeley and Los Angeles, California

University of California Press, Ltd.
London, England

The Library of Congress has cataloged an earlier edition
of this book as follows:

Library of Congress Cataloging-in-Publication Data

   Revising your dissertation : advice from leading editors /
edited by Beth Luey.
       p.   cm.
   Includes bibliographical references and index.

   ISBN 978-0-520-25401-5

   1. Dissertations, Academic.   2. Academic writing.   3.
Scholarly publishing.   I. Luey, Beth.

LB2369.R49   2004
808' .02—dc22   2004001717

Manufactured in the United States of America
16   15   14   13   12   11   10   09   08
10   9   8   7   6   5   4   3   2   1

CONTENTS

FOREWORD TO THE 2008 EDITION

At the time this volume was originally published, it was already becoming clear that the market for books based on dissertations was eroding. Twenty years ago, even ten years ago, there was no evidence to suggest that books based on dissertations were being discriminated against in purchases made by libraries through their approval plans with wholesale vendors like Yankee Book Peddler. But since the late 1990s it has become apparent that libraries do place such books in a special category.

The reason is simple and, from a librarian's standpoint, compelling. The traditional centralized repository of dissertations, University Microfilms (UMI), always had dissertations to sell, but demand for any one of them—photocopied in a small trim size with that ugly blue paper cover—was minuscule. As UMI evolved into ProQuest, however, they began storing dissertations electronically, and as the decade wore on, more and more universities began launching programs, often first voluntary and then mandatory, to have dissertations submitted in electronic form. A growing number of these universities joined the Networked Digital Library of Theses and Dissertations (http://www.ndltd.org), which cooperated in making dissertations available via "open access" (before the term was invented). Meanwhile, ProQuest was busy licensing its dissertation database to academic libraries throughout the world. The result of this natural evolution was that dissertations are now generally regarded as part of permanent library collections. Thus, the question inevitably arose for librarians, if we already have access to all these dissertations, why should we spend our strained book budget on revised dissertations? And so it came to pass that, according to Yankee Book Peddler, libraries began to ask their vendors to inspect the front matter of each book for any signs that it had its origin in a dissertation and, if such evidence was uncovered, to omit that book from the lot purchased through the approval plan.

University presses have responded, rationally according to their own perspective, by becoming more reluctant to publish books derived from dissertations. But they continue to publish them all the same, perhaps partly because editors like myself realize that some of the best and most influential books they have ever sponsored for publication have been just such first books based on dissertations. Let me give you just a few examples of books I edited that got their start as dissertations and proved, in revised form, to become pioneering works in their respective fields, catapulting their authors into the forefront of their disciplines: Sonia Alvarez's *Engendering Democracy in Brazil* (1990), Charles Beitz's *Political Theory and International Relations* (1979), Miguel Centeno's *Democracy within Reason* (1994), Susan Eckstein's *The Poverty of Revolution* (1977), Jean Bethke Elshtain's *Public Man, Private Woman* (1981), Peter Evans's *Dependent Development*

(1979), Helen Milner's *Resisting Protectionism* (1988), Susan Moller Okin's *Women and Western Political Thought* (1979), and Iris Marion Young's *Justice and the Politics of Difference* (1990). Alvarez and Eckstein have both served as president of the Latin American Studies Association; Centeno is director of the Princeton Institute for International and Regional Studies; Beitz and Milner also teach at Princeton; Evans is Professor of Sociology at University of California, Berkeley; and before their recent untimely deaths, Okin and Young were on the faculty, respectively, of Stanford and Chicago. One wonders what would have happened to their careers if they had not published such influential first books. I wonder the same for another person whose revised dissertation I published at Princeton in 1984: Condoleezza Rice. Would she be where she is today without that important first book, which helped her get tenure at Stanford, where she later became provost?

Last year an article appeared in the newsletter of the American Political Science Association giving advice to graduate students and junior faculty about publishing. Much of it was very good advice indeed, which I could heartily support. But the authors of this article included one recommendation that, while plausible at first glance, did not make sense in today's marketplace: they urged graduate students to write their dissertations as books to begin with, thus avoiding the extra step of revision. Taken in the larger context just described, this is very bad advice. There is now more than ever a premium on revising a dissertation substantially, in order to prove to librarians that the new book has sufficient "value added" to justify purchasing it. And for presses that are making their own decisions, the stakes have become higher ever since ProQuest announced late in 2005 that it had entered into a deal with Amazon to sell some dissertations through the online retailer. Editors must be persuaded that the revisions will make the book saleable in direct competition with the dissertation on Amazon!

The chapters in this volume will give everyone who pays close attention all the tools and ideas they need to transform a raw dissertation into a full-fledged book. Given the changes in the marketplace described above, authors may want to consider a few additional strategies: change the title of the dissertation so that the book is identifiable as something quite distinct; and either make no reference to its origin as a dissertation in the Acknowledgments at all, or else describe in some detail what changes were made to add value to the dissertation in the process of revision. Be prepared, in any event, for requests from editors to whom you submit your proposal for just such a detailed description. They will need to have it in order to persuade their press editorial boards that your book is indeed worth the investment of publishing it.

Sanford G. Thatcher
University Park, Pennsylvania
April 2007

IS THE PUBLISHABLE DISSERTATION
AN OXYMORON?

Beth Luey

Undergraduates consume knowledge. Scholars produce knowledge. Graduate school is the place where students make the transition from consumer to producer. There are exceptions, of course: Arthur M. Schlesinger Jr.'s first book began life as his undergraduate honors thesis. But most of college is spent in lectures, labs, and libraries learning what other people already know. In graduate school, passing qualifying exams or completing prescribed courses demonstrates that you have absorbed enough established knowledge to move on. Research seminars allow you to begin learning and communicating what others do *not* know. The dissertation is the culmination of this process: a significant original contribution to knowledge. Its publication as a book or in journals allows new knowledge to be disseminated to an audience beyond the doctoral committee.

This book was written for people at various stages in the dissertation process. It is directed mainly at those who have completed a dissertation and want to revise it for book publication, but it will be equally useful for those who have not yet begun the dissertation and want to make eventual revision and rewriting easier. Even those who are only beginning or contemplating graduate study should find valuable information here. The book should also be helpful to those who do not want to publish the dissertation as a book but rather wish to write journal articles based on their dissertation research and also to those who never want to look at their dissertation again (if only to justify that decision).

Why is revision necessary? Why can't graduate students just write books in the first place and call them dissertations? Alternatively, why can't graduate students just send their dissertations to publishers and have them recognized as books? The answers lie in the changing nature of scholarship and graduate education and in the changing economics of scholarly publishing.

The evolution from consumer to producer is also a shift from generalist to specialist. An undergraduate history major, for example, might be required to take courses in U.S., European, and non-Western history. A graduate student will specialize in, say, Asian history (with qualifying exams in one or two other fields) and will write a dissertation on a topic as narrow as a single doctrine of a single political group in one Chinese dynasty. This makes perfect sense. The purpose of the dissertation is to learn— and to demonstrate that you have learned—how to define an original topic, ask interesting questions, apply the relevant research skills and methodologies, tap the relevant resources, draw conclusions, and write about what you have learned. A student's first large, independent project has to be fairly narrow. Otherwise graduate school would consume decades rather than years.

What's wrong with writing a very careful study of a narrow topic for a small audience? Absolutely nothing. Narrowly focused scholarship can be excellent scholarship. In the hands of a skillful writer, it can even approach best-seller status. To stick with historians for a moment, think of Laurel Thatcher Ulrich's Pulitzer-winning *A Midwife's Tale*, a study based on the long-ignored diary of an obscure Maine midwife whose life spanned the eighteenth and nineteenth centuries. Some of Jonathan Spence's books have been similarly based on a single obscure figure or narrow topic. But Ulrich and Spence used their narrow foundations to build narrative mansions, moving from a specific life into geographically, temporally, and thematically larger arenas. These books did not begin as dissertations, but they could have: the initial topics were suitable for a thesis. A graduate student hasn't the time, the experience, or the breadth of vision of a senior scholar and is unlikely to produce a book with both exemplary scholarship and popular appeal. But young scholars can learn to make their work interesting to a larger audience by reading the work of those who do this with great skill. Reading good books will help you to write them.

Although writing on a narrow topic makes perfect sense when the goal is to complete a dissertation, *publishing* such work raises enormous problems. Even small nonprofit publishers must stay afloat and must justify their investment of time and money in one manuscript rather than another. Part of that justification lies in the quality of the work, but part also lies in the benefit to readers. A book that will appeal to a thousand readers is a better investment than one that will appeal to a hundred. It is more likely to influence a field of knowledge and advance work in that field. Some academic authors claim to be indifferent to sales, but this is foolish for two reasons. First, publishers do not and cannot share that indifference, and publishers determine what will become a book. Second, the book that is not sold is not read. Why bother writing if your work will have no influence on your colleagues? The value of a book is not in the lines it adds to your curriculum vitae but in the impact it has on your audience and on your discipline. (This is one reason why you may be reading this book even if you do not have a job in which you are expected to publish your dissertation. If you have done good, important work, others can benefit from it.)

In economic terms, a book that costs $30,000 to publish can be sold to a thousand readers at a price of around $50 (remember, the author gets a royalty and booksellers get a discount). If that book has only a hundred readers, it must be sold for around $500. Do you suppose there are a hundred scholars in your field who are likely to want your book that badly? There certainly aren't a hundred libraries.

In the past twenty years, university presses and other scholarly publishers have increased the number of titles they publish each year, but they have seen a dramatic drop in the number of copies of each book they can sell. That is one reason why the prices of scholarly books have increased. Library sales have fallen with library book budgets (victims of the cost of installing computers, buying more—and more expensive—journals, and acquiring such products as electronic databases, electronic subscriptions, and CD-ROMs), and narrowing fields of scholarship have fewer members, so each narrowly focused book has a smaller potential market among individual buyers. At the same time, the institutions that employ scholars expect more and more publication: in some fields, tenure requires at least one book, and at some institutions more than one is expected.

Technology has not solved the problem. Half the cost of a

scholarly book is overhead, which remains the same for electronic publications; the cost of paper, printing, and binding is relatively insignificant. Even if a book is not printed, it must be evaluated, edited, designed, and marketed. Users of electronic publications have high expectations for features like searchability, linked footnotes, and the like, whose creation takes time and money. Setting up and maintaining a Web site has significant costs. And no electronic format has the durability of acid-free paper. Unfortunately, it looks as if electronic books will be at least as expensive as ink on paper and may not last nearly as long. If electronic books could be made somewhat cheaper, the fact remains that people don't like to read whole books on a screen. Even Bill Gates prefers paper for anything over five pages. To make economic sense, electronic books—like their print equivalent—need a significant body of readers willing to pay a fair price.

Perhaps you can now see why a dissertation is not a book. If you want to get out of graduate school in a reasonable amount of time, you are well advised to choose a narrow topic. If you want to publish a book, you need a manuscript with wider appeal. A publishable dissertation is beginning to sound like an oxymoron. It isn't, though, and this book will help you understand why not. You need to think about a larger audience and how you can appeal to a greater variety of readers. The basic trick is to choose a narrow, manageable topic that can be opened up, broadened, and extended into something that many more people will want to read. Beyond that, you need to learn to write differently, beginning with organization and moving on to voice, style, and language. Avoiding jargon is only the beginning; you need to develop an appropriate personal style and voice. And you need to modify the apparatus of scholarship for your new, larger audience.

MANAGING GRADUATE SCHOOL

Whole books and administrative careers have been devoted to figuring out how to make graduate education work, and I will not plunge into that morass. However, looking at graduate school as an experience that should prepare you to become a successful academic author provides insight into some larger questions.

Many students decide to attend graduate school in order to write a dissertation on a topic that has long fascinated them. They choose the department with the scholar most likely to be helpful on that topic, giving little thought to the rest of the graduate experience, and they see qualifying exams (or their equivalent) as an inconvenient obstacle. This approach practically guarantees that graduate school will yield little value and less fun. You must, of course, have a fairly firm idea of the field in which you wish to work in order to choose a graduate department strong in the area. You should also make sure the faculty members in that field are compatible with one another and with you. If you choose the most prestigious academic mentor available and then discover that you are ideologically or personally incompatible, you will either fail to complete your degree or complete it only after extraordinary discomfort or seismic changes in your plans.

You will be better off, though, if you are receptive to many ideas about possible dissertations. In other words, begin graduate school with an open mind and stay curious. Your own interests may change, or someone else may complete the definitive work on your subject while you are preparing for your exams. You may discover that the archival material you need has been closed to researchers. You may come across material far more interesting to you than what you had planned to work on. As you take courses and do independent reading, you may find a far better topic than the one you began with. And acquiring some insight into what scholarly publishers consider important in selecting what to publish, which this book will provide, may help you to define your interests in a more productive way.

You should choose your courses systematically, with one eye on passing qualifying exams according to schedule and the other on exploring dissertation topics and perhaps even making progress on research and writing. Your reading for courses and exams can also be used to develop a mental file of possible models for your own research and writing, as well as to discover research avenues for possible articles and future projects. Try to work with a variety of faculty members early on so that you get to know the people who might serve on your dissertation committee and learn about research areas you haven't yet explored thoroughly. Students in the humanities and social sciences should take courses that make them read good books and do a lot of writing. Students in the sciences should take courses that require writing up research as they would for publication, and they should seek out research experiences that allow them to participate in the writing as well as the research. As you begin to focus on possible dissertation topics, you may be able to use coursework to get started on background reading for the dissertation, methodology, and even some research. One of my colleagues advises students to use their research seminars to get started on dissertation chapters, and those who are able to do so begin well ahead of people who have been less systematic. Do not follow this advice until you have finished your exploration and experimentation, though. Don't even think about starting on your dissertation, in any form, in your first year.

Some departments include courses in professional practice that discuss the process of readying papers for oral presentation and journal submission and give students experience in these matters. Others offer such preparation in workshops. Take advantage of these even if they are not required. If such formal guidance is not available, find faculty members who will provide informal guidance. Your fellow graduate students, especially those who have been around for a few years, may act as though these are things that *everyone* knows. They didn't know them when they arrived, and quite possibly they still do not. Don't be embarrassed to admit you need help.

Your department, and departments with similar intellectual interests, will sponsor many presentations of research by resident faculty, visitors, and job applicants. Attend as many of these as you can. Ask visitors how they selected their topics and how they developed their ideas. Pay attention not only to the talks but to the responses they evoke. You can learn about other people's research but also about how to present your work—and how not to.

If you have a graduate assistantship or fellowship, try to work with faculty who will help you. In your first year you will probably have little choice about your assignment, but start scouting around for better opportunities in the following year. Let faculty members know that you are interested in working with them. Especially in a large department, you may have to make an effort to get to know professors even a little outside your major field. An especially enlightening experience is working with a journal editor.

The main consideration in choosing members for your committee is, of course, their areas of interest. Especially at the dissertation stage, though, you should learn something about their writing. Read what faculty members have written, even if it is not assigned, looking not only at what they write but also at how they write. Find at least one person for your committee whose writing you would like to emulate, even if that person may turn out to be somewhat peripheral to the focus of your dissertation.

Early in your graduate career, learn about possible sources of research support from professional organizations, funding agencies, foundations, and your own university. If you are able to find funding for your research over the summers, or even for a year or two of writing, you will finish your work more quickly and be able to take advantage of many more resources than will otherwise be available to you. Attend proposal-writing workshops and seek the advice of faculty members who are successful in gaining grants. Funding is not the only advantage of getting grants. The process helps you articulate your ideas, brings outside advice, and makes others in your field aware of your work; success validates both your project and your ability to carry it out. This will be helpful when you apply for jobs and when you submit work for publication.

Take advantage of opportunities to present papers on your work at conferences and departmental colloquia. Your first attempts may be in local or regional settings, but these are good preparation for the larger audiences that you will seek out later. Giving papers in any setting helps to shape your ideas and to put you in touch with people who share your interests. It may generate ideas for future work, disclose the whereabouts of missing evidence, and be useful in other ways.

Your graduate career should be as short as possible, but long enough to allow you to prepare adequately for the next stage in your professional life and to take advantage of what is offered. Graduate school is generally not the high point of anyone's life, and those who may want to hire you will pay attention to how long it has taken you to get your degree. However, the way to keep it short is not to rush through wearing blinders. Instead, try to make the most of the intellectual and practical resources available to you. Think of yourself as a Labrador lolloping through a field full of interesting sights, sounds, and smells rather than as a greyhound on a racetrack. As long as you are within a year of the average time to degree in your discipline, you shouldn't worry.

USING THIS BOOK

Each of the contributors to this volume has a wealth of experience with books of all kinds, including books that began as dissertations. Each has different practical suggestions for making the task of revision easier, but they all share certain convictions. The first is that the wise author focuses on readers. Although the first chapter's topic is specifically the audience, nearly every contributor talks about readers. Who will want to read your book? How can you make it interesting to more people? You want to reach the largest audience possible, but to have an opportunity to do that, you must first impress a single reader: the acquiring editor at a university press. Most contributors to this volume have tried to share the view from their desks, to help you understand the questions they are asking when they read your proposal or manuscript. Editors are a surrogate for the audience. They know which of their books have succeeded and have a pretty good idea why. When they read proposals, they evaluate them in the light of their past experience as well as their taste and knowledge of the subject matter.

The second shared conviction is that the wise author reads

widely and learns from that reading. As a researcher you read to understand methodology and content, but as a writer you should read to understand technique and style. Find well-written books in your specialty but outside your subspecialty, and see how the authors make their ideas clear to a broadened base of readers. If you are a political scientist who has written about Argentina, look for books in political science that deal with Latin America generally. Alternatively, you might read books about Argentina that deal with politics but also with other aspects of society and culture. This kind of reading will also help you understand what editors mean by "voice." Good books sound as if they were written by a human being, and the author's voice is what creates this quality.

The third shared conviction is that the wise author seeks advice and learns to follow it. It is easy to understand why a young scholar, after years of doing nothing but listening to advice from the faculty, might glory in newfound independence. But even the most senior scholar can benefit from the opinions of others. Authors revising dissertations should seek the advice of colleagues in their own institutions and beyond. They should take advantage of whatever resources their universities offer: many now organize workshops on authorship, grant seeking, and the like conducted by senior scholars from a variety of departments. Editors, too, will offer advice—their own and that of peer reviewers. It's important to learn how to accept praise, criticism, and suggestions.

One key element in revising a dissertation is creativity. Do not imagine that you can simply go through your work line by line and fix things, or just take out a section or paragraph here and there. You need to rethink your work, to look at it with a fresh eye and see how it could be made more interesting and valuable to more people. This rethinking may lead to reshaping your topic, reorganizing your material, and providing an entirely new narrative framework.

The final bit of shared wisdom is not to revise immediately but to let the dissertation sit for a while. The tenure clock may be ticking, but leaving the manuscript on the shelf for a few months will work to your benefit. You can spend that time reading good books and getting ideas, both for revising your book and for developing other projects. You may also decide, in the course of these weeks, that the dissertation has served its purpose and you would rather work on something else. If you take a job where publication is not required, that is an easy choice. If you are expected to publish, though, you should make that decision only if it is clear that your dissertation cannot be turned into a worthwhile book or that you have absolutely no further interest in it. In that case, you need to get started on another project—one that will sustain your interest and end up as a publishable piece of work. You also need to see what parts of the dissertation can easily be reworked into journal articles, because there is no reason to let all that work go to waste. Even in fields where book publication is expected, candidates for tenure (and sometimes first jobs) are expected to have published an article or two. In some fields, several substantial articles are adequate.

In the first section of this book, we provide advice that will be useful to all our readers. Contributors to the second section have focused on certain areas of scholarship. The chapter on your own area is likely to be most useful, but you may want to read some of the others as well. For example, no matter what field you are writing in, if your book has more than an illustration or two, you will want to read Judy Metro's chapter on the arts. Or if your degree is in psychology, you may not have considered the possibility of writing for clinicians rather than scholars. Be sure to read Johanna Von-deling's chapter on professional books before you make up your mind. And no matter what your field, if some of your dissertation work should be published in journals, you will find Trevor Lip-scombe's chapter on the sciences useful.

To get your degree, you may have had to develop some habits that you now must unlearn. For example, with a Ph.D. in hand you rise to the higher end of the evolutionary scale that ranges from student to mentor, which requires new attitudes and behavior. On the whole, though, graduate school has prepared you for a life of scholarship. You have a sound grasp of the methods and knowledge of a broad discipline, as well as a specialist's insights into a narrower field. You know how to prepare and present papers, apply for fund-ing and jobs, teach undergraduates about your field and inspire their interest in it, and write about your work in a way that makes it clear and interesting to your peers. None of these skills—re-search, speaking, teaching, and writing—is learned once and for-ever, and they are not just collections of techniques. They are arts that scholars develop and refine over many years. Your dissertation was the end of graduate school. Your first book is the beginning of a lifetime of learning and sharing knowledge.

PART I

RETHINKING AND REVISING

1

YOU'RE THE AUTHOR NOW

William P. Sisler

OK, so you've passed your orals, defended your thesis success-fully, gotten your union card. So far, so good. But the pressure is intense and immediate. To get ahead, to stay ahead, you need to get that book out. You have the raw material, but it's not a book; it's a dissertation, and that won't do. Why? Because when you wrote your thesis, you were an acolyte not yet empowered to speak with authority and gravitas. Now, as you begin to think about moving that dissertation into book mode, you'll need to make a gestalt shift, in which you stop seeing yourself as a suppli-cant seeking to convince the chosen few (your dissertation com-mittee) and start seeing yourself as a creator, an expert, an au-thority—an author.

As an author—as *the* author—you've taken charge of your work; you have a right to speak and be heard. Your readers will pick up your book not to judge your mastery of the facts or your facility with the literature in your field but to learn something new. Unlike your dissertation committee, they will assume you know what you're talking about. Still, your readers don't want to learn everything you know: they want to know what you *think*. They want to hear your opinion in your voice, not what all those other authorities you've read and quoted had to say. And they don't want a tour of the side streets, byways, and alleys discovered in your research. They only want to know what's relevant to the argument at hand.

It's one thing to assert your right to your own voice and quite another to know what that voice actually is. Most of us are pretty good mimics—we can write a paragraph that reads like the *New York Times* or the *Daily News;* we can imitate the cadences of an Al Gore or a George Bush. But when it comes to sounding like *ourselves*, we're at a loss.

To get past this first writer's block, try asking yourself who your ideal readers truly are. Are you planning a monograph, written at a very high level, for experts alone? Nothing wrong with that. But the tone of your tome will change suddenly if instead you imagine yourself lecturing to a classroom of college sophomores or, widening the circle further, envision yourself as the host of a PBS special, speaking plainly and simply to the interested viewer. In reality, these are not mutually exclusive cadres, but for the purpose of finding your voice, it helps to focus on one particular type of reader. Better yet, instead of imagining a roomful of experts or sophomores or neighbors, try thinking about one particular person you want to persuade and tell your story to that reader. The person could be the history professor down the hall or that lawyer you just met downtown—pick your own target and then ask yourself how to hit it. What kind of words and phrases would you use to talk with this person about this topic? Sentence fragments? Maybe a few. Rhetorical questions? Many writers use them to good effect. Second person? That's for you to decide.

Whether your intended reader is a member of academe or of the general trade audience, you need to read your writing out loud, to see how it sounds in your ear and feels in your mouth. If you can't imagine speaking those words to that particular person, then choose different words. As every parent knows, reading aloud can teach quite a bit about good writing. Simpler is better—we've known that since *Goodnight, Moon*. Shorter is better, too. The manifold temptations of the word processor should be resisted. It's simply too easy now to go on and on, adding more and more, shuffling every metaphorical index card to stack that deck higher and higher in your favor. But think again of your reader. What does that reader need to know about your subject and your take on it? The reason someone will read your book is to benefit from your distillation of years spent in research. Readers don't want to experience the tedium of your years in the stacks, the archives, or the lab; they seek the value of your expertise. A few years back a well-known scholar made the case for the hypertext book, arguing that the electronic format would create a "pyramid" allowing the reader to follow the scholar down to the lowest levels, to track with the scholar through the subterranean labyrinths of years of endeavor, and to relive the "joys" of discovery. Forget it! Life's too short! Your reader wants to be at the top of the pyramid, mastering the big picture, not dusting down below for hieroglyphics.

But let's step back for a minute and focus on just what your book is about. What is the appeal of your subject? Sure, it was interesting enough for you to spend considerable time and energy on it and significant enough for your committee to grant you a degree, but will your topic appeal in its current guise, first to an acquisitions editor who has a limited amount of time and a limited number of publishing slots to fill, then to the external reviewers, and finally to a sufficient number of potential readers to justify the publisher's investment? Can you broaden its appeal by spending some more time on research to extend the work chronologically (why end in 1956 instead of bringing it up to the present?), geographically (why limit it to the Western world?), by adding other texts (not just *Goodnight, Moon,* but *Pat the Bunny* and *The Very Hungry Caterpillar*), or cultures, or characters? What limits did you and your advisers put on the scale and scope of your project to enable you to contain it and finish it? What trails did you not follow that you'd now like to pursue to broaden and deepen your argument? Did you write on Dante's *Inferno?* Should you extend your argument to the entire *Divine Comedy?* (OK, maybe not.) But if you've analyzed a single play by Marlowe, or Jonson, or even Shakespeare, your chances for getting a book accepted these days are slim. You need to make a larger statement with more examples and a thesis that will cover more ground. Think again of your reader and what new angles, or players, or histories, or examples will increase the appeal of your work. Then think of yourself. What kind of book do you like to read, whether for professional development or for pleasure, and how does your original or current version match up? What criticisms and tips from your dissertation advisers or other readers are worth adding to the mix now that your defense is over? Think of this question as you develop the work: Who needs this book and why? More crassly, who'll spend thirty bucks (or more) to read what you've written?

You need a systematic approach to find the book within the

thesis, or to develop the book from the thesis, and to create a work that will cry out for a place in the publisher's list at a time when the competition is becoming more and more intense. Let's begin at the beginning, with the title. The title is first and foremost a marketing tool, and you want to choose one that will instantly grab the attention of the overworked editor on whose desk your proposal will land. Now, unless you have perfect pitch, are very lucky, or have a crystal-clear subject, odds are that the title of the published book will be different from what you submit anyway, but at this point you want a grabber to pull your work out of the undifferentiated pile. It probably should be accurate, maybe even descriptive, certainly not poetic and flowery. But try not to make it dull and formulaic. Here are some genuine titles that capture one's attention (as Dave Barry would say, "I am not making this up"): *Who's Who in Barbed Wire*; *Defensive Tactics with Flashlights*; *Lappish Bear Graves in Northern Sweden*; *All about Mud*; *Hypnotizing Animals*; *Stress and Fish* (all from *Bizarre Books*, by Russell Ash and Brian Lake, published by Pavilion Books in 1998). Would you have picked up this book if it were titled something like *Thesis and Antithesis*, or *Booking a Career*, or *Gathering the Winds: Reaping the Rewards of Writing?* Probably not.

Next, look at the chapter titles. Do they convey solid information about what's in the text? Are they long, dull, cute, punning? In most cases, cute and punning will not do. Should the book be structured in parts? If you feel the table of contents and the book itself need additional subheads, these should be consistent with the tone and subject of your topic. Too many subheads can give a choppy feeling to the book and its argument and can be offputting in the table of contents. You may indeed have needed these as structural supports while you were writing, but now that the writing is finished, they should go. Unless you're engaged in a technical philosophical analysis or scientific treatise, avoid plentiful subheads. Think of the table of contents as the second most important page in the book after the title. It's the skeleton of your book, on which the body will develop. It's also your opportunity to lay out for the reader how the book will evolve, and therefore it's crucial to have the chapter and part titles (if any) work together.

You've chosen a good title, created a clear and accurate table of contents, and composed solid chapter titles. Now to open the text proper that you've whittled (or expanded) from the original dissertation.

The opening, most often an introduction, is your first real opportunity to engage the reader. Does your subject allow you to begin with an anecdote, a historical occurrence, or the establishment of your main character's identity, as in "When the posse arrived at Margarita Chacon's house at 11 P.M. on this rainy night, George Frazer, superintendent of the copper smelter, banged on the door with the butt of his Winchester"? Or is your subject best introduced plainly and simply, as in "Seldom do we reflect upon what philosophy is in itself"? In either case the object is to gain the attention of your readers, draw them in, keep them reading, and stimulate their desire to keep going with the story. The opening is your appetizer, offering a savory taste to prepare them for the banquet of your ideas. If it's too dense and heavy, the reader may be sated before the main course. The introduction should be consistent with your title and table of contents in tone and approach. It should lead naturally into the body of the book.

But let's not forget that the body has to be in shape, and for most of us, that means losing a little weight. If you've written a massive piece of scholarship, including every bit of evidence for your thesis, every reference, every bibliographical flag, every brick in the defensive wall to keep out those Inquisitors challenging your right to the Doctors' lounge, it's now time to follow Mae West, who said, "Between two evils, I always pick the one I never tried before." Try the shorter route. Begin by eliminating the review of the literature, if you have one. Your audience assumes you're an authority; you don't need to establish your bona fides. Chop the methodological bits. The reader doesn't need to know the fine points of how you got to your destination. She wants the panoramic view when she arrives with you. If you really do have some innovative and groundbreaking methodologies, consider working them up into a journal article or articles for the cognoscenti. Is the text peppered with infighting, attacks on other scholars, skirmishes that only the illuminati will appreciate? Byebye. Look with a gimlet eye on those footnotes, and if they're discursive, either bring them into the text proper or eliminate them. And that bibliography? Let it go. But if you feel you really must retain it, pare it to its most essential elements. Appendices? You'd best have a very good reason for keeping them in. As Thoreau said, "Simplify, simplify." (So why'd he say it twice?) Your audience will thank you, and your publisher will smile more kindly upon you.

2

WHAT IS YOUR BOOK ABOUT?

Beth Luey

By the time students finish graduate school, they may react fairly violently to the question, What is your dissertation about? Every relative, new graduate student, and casual acquaintance asks, and the wise job candidate has one-minute, five-minute, and forty-minute answers for interviews. Now you have to figure out what your *book* is about, and the answer had better not be the same. Chapter 1 talked about audience, so you know that the people asking the question will be both more numerous than and quite different from those who asked about your dissertation. They will be, first, book editors and then—if the editors like your answer—readers. Your description of the dissertation was meant to tell other scholars in your subfield that you were doing important work, asking the right questions, reading the right authorities, applying the right theories and methodologies, and tapping the right sources of evidence. Your description of your book has to tell the editor and future readers that you have something interesting to say which is worth their time—even if they know very little about the narrow area of your work. Methodology, theory, and earlier interpretations are of little—if any—interest to them. To broaden your audience, you must provide context and background (which your dissertation readers did not need) and recast your topic so that readers will want to open the book and keep turning the pages.

The way you go about this will depend on your starting point—the dissertation itself—as well as the resources for expansion. Almost any topic can be made interesting and accessible if you have unlimited time and resources, but that is never the case. In deciding how to expand your topic, you will need to look at what other scholars have written that you might draw on, at the unused material you have on hand, at what new research you can reasonably undertake in the amount of time available, and at what interests you. As the following fictional examples show, every topic might be turned into one of several books. You can work out the possibilities for your topic, narrow the choices to those that are feasible, and then choose the one that is most interesting to you. You may also wish to consult others—including colleagues and editors—about which course to take. You will notice that some of these topics, whether by luck or design, lend themselves more readily to revision for a broader audience. If you have not yet chosen a topic, you might keep that in mind.

RIPE FOR REVISION

I have fabricated a number of possible dissertations. Some of them are very interesting to me, while others would put me to sleep in short order. In each case, though, I have tried to come up with several books that might be written with the dissertation as a beginning, books that I would look at seriously if they came across my desk. I have also noted some of the problems that the authors would need to consider as they planned their revisions.

John Doe: A Political Biography

This well-written history dissertation provides a detailed analysis of Doe's political career, covering major legislation and issues tackled as well as election campaigns. The author used extensive archival sources (all of Doe's official and personal papers are open and in a nearby library), as well as newspaper accounts and interviews with some of Doe's surviving colleagues and aides. The dissertation is organized chronologically. It places Doe in the context of other politicians of his era and shows how his political ideas developed over the course of his life. Unless Doe was a well-known political figure—a president, a nationally known member of Congress, or a big-city mayor—this dissertation will not be a successful book without substantial revision. Fortunately the material for revision is readily available, so all the author needs is a plan.

The most obvious route to take is to transform the dissertation into a full-fledged biography—not just the official life but also the personal life, the life before, after, and outside politics. Is this possible? The personal papers are available in the archives, and it may still be possible to interview colleagues and friends about unofficial matters. Equally important, was Doe's life interesting? If he had no life outside politics, this is a nonstarter. But if he did, will it hold the reader's interest? Might it help us understand his political life? For example, can you trace his lifelong interest in health care issues to the death of siblings or children? Was he likable or loathsome? A yes to either is good; bland is a problem. An editor once pointed out that all biographies end the same way. Because there are no surprise endings, the key to judging a biography is whether you care when the subject dies. If you don't, the book doesn't work. A perfect subject for both a dissertation and an expanded biography would be Jimmy Carter (though he is still very much alive). The political biography would be brief and manageable and therefore appropriate for a dissertation; the full life would be a salable and fascinating book.

If you know that, beyond his work, your subject was boring, you need to do something different. Can you develop Senator Doe's involvement in one important issue into a book about that issue and its legislative history? If he was the mayor of a big city where racial tensions were resolved without violence, can you write about his role in race relations but add the dimensions of community, police, schools, and other individuals and institutions? This would give your book strong regional interest as well as national possibilities. Or can you compare his handling of race relations with that of other mayors facing the same issues at the same time? If Doe was involved in any major event, issue, or conflict, you might do well to refocus your study away from the person and onto the issue.

None of these options is unrealistic in terms of the amount of work to be done, provided that sources are available. Doe need not have been the central actor in the story, but he must at least have played a major supporting role. Some very bad books have resulted from exaggerating the importance of the author's favorite character. You would need to tell your readers enough about the city, the issue, or the event to draw them into the story and to provide the background they need to understand the book. The rest of your task would be learning to tell the story in an exciting way.

And a stripped-down version of the political biography would make an impressive journal article.

Afghan Women under the Taliban: A Village Study

A clearly imaginary, but very fortunate, anthropology student spent a year in a small village in Afghanistan observing the impact of Taliban rule on the women of the community. The result was a detailed study of a small group of women in unusual and extreme circumstances. Even though political events have called the world's attention to the plight of women under the Taliban regime, this study is too narrow, specialized, and technical to succeed as a book. It is burdened with anthropological theory and jargon. Fortunately, the author has a number of ways to make her work publishable.

One possibility is to expand the study geographically beyond Afghanistan, comparing the community in her study to others of similar size in fundamentalist Islamic societies in other countries. Using the data in published studies of such groups (assuming that they exist), she can ask the same questions she asked of her own data. She would have to provide her readers with enough background in Islamic theology and history to understand why these are the right questions to ask and why the answers matter. The book would be, not a community study, but a study of contemporary Islamic women in small communities. Whatever theory the author found useful and productive would undergird the study, but the girders would be well hidden beneath layers of vivid description and human stories.

Another possibility, if travel funds are available, would be to expand the study temporally. What happened to the community and its women when the Taliban regime was overthrown? This option, if successfully executed, would have editors battling for the book. It has enormous appeal and interest. Its ultimate success, again, would depend on its humanity.

Yet another choice would be to expand the topic culturally, looking at women in comparable communities with governments composed of fundamentalists of other religions. This would be the most difficult conceptually, but the material would probably be available and the book would be interesting to a variety of scholars and might be used in women's studies and religious studies classes.

No matter which of these options the author chose, she would have to abandon the detached, scientific approach to the material that she took in the dissertation in favor of a more personal approach that revealed her own interactions with the women she studied, her responses to them, and their attitudes toward her. Theory would be subordinated to narrative. Some theoretical material, though, could probably be worked into a journal article.

The Impact of Immigration on a Public High School

The author received his doctorate in education by writing this dissertation, a case study of a high school whose population was rapidly diversified by immigration during a ten-year period. He studied the demography of the neighborhood and the school, the impact of various school board policies, changes in test scores and other outcomes, and changes in curriculum and extracurricular activities. It is a timely topic, of much interest, but it's just one high school and much of what he addresses is not of interest to anyone except academics in schools of education. There are far too many statistics, tables, and graphs to hold the attention of most readers. Yet there are at least two ways to make this dissertation into a book.

First, the author might branch out in his methodology. To statistics and demographics, he could add studies of teacher and student attitudes, elicited through surveys and interviews. He might spend some time on campus, observing students and teachers firsthand. He could refine his statistical studies to look more closely at the different immigrant groups that make up the new population of the school. He might look at other variables, such as language abilities and race. He might look at actions the school took, or failed to take, to improve relations among various groups. He might focus on one dramatic episode that brought these issues to the fore. The methodology would not be described in the book, though some of the studies might make good journal articles. The statistics would be summarized and humanized with examples of (appropriately disguised) specific students. The result might be a book of interest to readers concerned with the dynamics of communities in transition. If written differently, it might be a book for high school principals and school administrators seeking to deal with demographic change.

Alternatively, he might use his study as a springboard for a discussion of political issues related to immigration and education, such as bilingual education, school choice, school funding, and charter schools. He would have to use studies of other schools, and he would have to develop the ability to express political views cogently and persuasively. If sharply argued, this book would have enormous potential. The original dissertation would be unrecognizable, reduced to the source of the author's convictions and a few telling examples.

Shortly after I made up this example, I came across the following catalogue description for *Race in the Schoolyard*, published in May 2003 by Rutgers University Press. The author, Amanda E. Lewis, received her Ph.D. in 2000 and is an assistant professor at the University of Illinois at Chicago:

> *Race in the Schoolyard* takes us to a place most of us seldom get to see in action—our children's classrooms—and reveals the lessons about race that are communicated there. The author spent a year at three elementary schools . . . observing in school classrooms, yards, and lunchrooms. The book shows that the curriculum (expressed and hidden) teaches many racial lessons, and that schools and their personnel serve as a means of both affirming and challenging previous racial attitudes and understanding. . . . The book describes racialized moments in a setting where race is purported not to matter. These are moments that educational statistics cannot capture.

The book has been issued in cloth and paper, suggesting that the press expects it to sell far more than most monographs would.

You're Giving Me Ulcers

Although doctors believed for many years that ulcers were caused by stress, it turns out that stress is less important than the presence of a common bacterium. An inexpensive antibiotic works wonders. A graduate student in the history of medicine thought, correctly, that this would be a good dissertation topic. She focused on the way that medical and scientific opinion shifted and why that shift was so protracted and difficult. This allowed her to demonstrate her understanding of the history and philosophy of science. But she now wants to write a book that will reach a larger audience—an audience less interested in the process of changing scientific opinion and more interested in . . . ? She has a lot of possibilities.

First, she might look at medical economics. How did the new understanding of the cause of ulcers affect the sale of ulcer medications, and how did the industry respond? To what extent did the vested interests of the pharmaceutical industry and of doctors impede research into bacteriological causation? This would take her into policy issues and would require an understanding of economics that she might not have. And although it would be an interesting and valuable book, it would not have as broad an interest as other alternatives.

Perhaps instead she might look at how the attitudes of doctors and patients, as well as the larger culture, change when a disease ceases to be seen as primarily psychosomatic. The medical literature would provide a great deal of evidence, and she might also interview some of the doctors involved in the reformulation of treatment, who might in turn direct her to patients willing to discuss their experiences. Evidence about patient and general cultural attitudes would come from the same sources but also from cartoons and fiction. This reformulation of her topic would allow her to discuss more general issues, including our understanding of the mind and the body. Such a book would attract a great deal of interest.

The approach that would be closest to her training would involve expanding the topic to other diseases that have moved from the psychosomatic to the somatic. Such a book would remain in the realm of history of medicine, but it would also—if properly written—attract nonspecialist readers. This would work only if there were such diseases and if they were well enough documented.

Will Singing Make Your Baby Smarter?

A graduate student in educational psychology wrote his dissertation about the "Mozart effect," whose proponents claim that listening to classical music improves children's cognitive abilities. He tested the theory in a local preschool and elementary school, in a series of very well designed experiments. It was an excellent dissertation and advanced the work done in this field significantly. He has already published a couple of journal articles based on his work. Now he wants to write a book. Like his colleague who chose ulcers as a topic, he has chosen a subject that lends itself easily to a number of book treatments.

First, he might write a book about the search for quick fixes in education and child rearing. Listening to classical music is just one in a series of activities that have been recommended to parents seeking more intelligent offspring. Many of them, including listening to Mozart, have some benefits, but none of them is adequate in itself. Why are American parents so eager to enhance their children's intellectual abilities, yet also eager to believe that this can be done effortlessly? This would require an understanding of attitudes toward parenting far beyond what he learned in writing the dissertation, but it would repay the effort. Somewhere down the road (after tenure) he might transform what he learned into a parenting book for an even larger market.

Another possibility would be to set his study in the context of the role of imagination, creativity, and the arts in education. Why are these subjects important? What do they contribute to children's growth? How can they best be nurtured? Again, this takes him far beyond the dissertation, but presumably he has an interest in arts education or he would not have chosen this subject. Again, such a book might be recast for parents later on.

Finally, he might decide to turn his research to a practical use and write a book about the value of arts education that is directed at arts groups attempting to influence public policy and at those who formulate educational policy. His own research and that of others will show the benefits, and these can be described in ways that both arts lobbyists and educational administrators can understand readily.

FREEING YOUR IMAGINATION

Most people who are writing a dissertation, or who have recently finished one, are far too wrapped up in it to be able to analyze its potential for development. But there are some tricks you might try to help you generate ideas. The one that's the most fun is to pretend you are a guest on an intelligent talk show—*Fresh Air* or *Charlie Rose*, perhaps—and the host wants to talk to you about your dissertation. Terry Gross and Charlie Rose have an amazing talent for digging out what is interesting in their guests' work. Try to imagine the on-air conversation:

TERRY GROSS: Our guest this afternoon has written a political biography of John Doe, who was mayor of Yourtown in the 1960s and 1970s. You know, Bill, as I read your dissertation, I was fascinated by the fact that the racial tensions in Yourtown were resolved without violence. Why do you think that happened?

CHARLIE ROSE: I'd like to welcome Myrna Luckout, who has written a study of the women in a small Afghan village under the Taliban regime. Myrna, will you be able to return to Afghanistan to see how the lives of these women have changed now that the Taliban is no longer in power?

TERRY GROSS: George, most people assume that when a school suddenly finds itself with a student body speaking two dozen languages, from even more cultures, this is an enormous educational problem. Yet in the school you studied, test scores and other measures of academic achievement actually improved as the school population became more diverse. Why do you think that happened?

CHARLIE ROSE: Kim, we've all seen those 1950s cartoons and advertisements about corporate executives getting ulcers because of the pressures of their jobs. Now it turns out that an ordinary little germ was causing all that angst. Why did it take so long to figure that out?

TERRY GROSS: Glenn, you have been looking at whether parents and teachers can make children smarter by having them listen to classical music. This seems kind of odd. What made people try this in the first place?

I have never heard Terry Gross or Charlie Rose interview anyone about a dissertation, so you'll have to use your imagination. But you can see how this might get you to focus on what is really interesting, new, and worth developing in your own work.

If you cannot imagine being interviewed on radio or television, you might try a more mechanical approach. Begin with the most specific description of your topic that you can formulate:

Women in a Taliban-controlled Afghan village in 1999

Now take each component and see how many ways you can generalize it:

women: people
Taliban: Islamic fundamentalists, religious fundamentalists
Afghan village: Afghan community, Islamic community
1999: 1999 to the present

Some of these will be dead ends. For example, our anthropologist studied women in the Afghan village, and she has neither data about nor access to the male community. But others suggest new ways to look at the material and might be productive.

Yet another possibility is simply to ask yourself what interested you about your topic in the first place. Perhaps that got lost in the academic exercise but can now be brought back to life. Alternatively, perhaps you abandoned that interest long ago and it makes more sense to ask what you'd like to look at next and how the research you have already done can support your new interests.

PLOT, CHARACTER, AND SETTING

No, you are not writing a novel. But all the elements of fiction can be injected into your work to make it interesting to more people. Indeed, some of them will have to be. For *plot*, read *narrative*. You should think of your book as telling a story. It should have a beginning, a middle, an end, and something must move it along that trajectory. It may be chronological or not, but there has to be some organizational logic and some impelling force that keeps your audience reading. All the elements of a plot may already be present in your story, but in the dissertation they have been subordinated to theory, methodology, or detail. Now the plot has to be brought to the front and developed dramatically. If possible, you should create some suspense about how it turns out. (The exception to this is the book that is meant to be immediately useful to professional or other readers, which should not contain surprises.)

Character is essential to most books. *Humanize* your subject. If your work is in the humanities or social sciences, this should not be difficult. Although the people may have gotten lost in the theory, methodology, or statistics, they are still there and can be brought to life. Sometimes they need to be brought front and center; at other times, they can just be illustrative examples. But they must be there. In the sciences, journal articles don't need plot, character, or setting. They are written according to a well-established formula. But if you want to write a *book* in the sciences, you will probably have to add material about the history of the field, the personalities involved in various discoveries, or the impact of the work on human lives. Our historian will humanize his study of John Doe by making it a full-fledged biography; the Afghan women will come alive in the revised dissertation, as will the children and teachers in the high school; the ulcer researchers and patients will play a prominent role; and real children and parents will be incorporated into the book about music.

Another way that writers humanize their subject is to inject their own personality into the narrative. This is the way that Stephen Hawking, John Kenneth Galbraith, and Steven Pinker became household words. This alternative takes great confidence and the ability to write personally without being obnoxious. It is probably not a good choice for your first book, but you might want to experiment a bit anyway.

For many books, the physical setting is an important element. In the fictional examples, readers would want to know what Doe's city looked like and where it was, and they would want to be able to visualize the landscape and street plan of the Afghan village and the style of its houses.

NEXT STEPS

Once you have decided on the direction your revision will take, write a paragraph describing the book you hope to write, just for yourself (see "Planning Tools" for further suggestions). What is Terry Gross's question? How will you answer it? Who is your audience? What is your plot, and what keeps it moving? Who are the main characters? When that is done, you are ready to plan further research and reading. Once you have found the material you need, it is time to think about conceptualizing and organizing your book, as Scott Norton describes in the next chapter.

WASTE NOT, WANT NOT

As you refocus your work to write a book, you will throw out a lot of words and work. Even when you wrote the dissertation, you probably had to leave out some interesting, useful information and set aside some intriguing questions and ideas. Before you discard anything, look into the possibility of recycling. Some of that material can be turned into journal articles.

For example, you may have come up with some innovative methodology that doesn't belong in the book but would make a very publishable article. The authors of the imaginary dissertations about high school and Mozart could probably write one or two articles of this kind. Our biographer might take an episode of John Doe's life that does not deserve lengthy treatment in the book and develop it more fully as an article. In some cases, this will require some additional reading or research, but usually not much. You should not try to extract material from the book itself for articles: book publishers are not interested in reprinting journal articles.

Another possibility is that, once you have removed the literature review and methodology, you have enough material for one or two very solid journal articles rather than a book. University press editors have a very good eye for padding, and if you have stretched an article out into a book, you are likely to experience many rejections. To acknowledge that your first book will *not* be a revision of your dissertation takes a good deal of courage and the confidence that you can write a book from scratch in time for tenure review, but this may be the better course. The Modern Language Association and the American Historical Association have been discussing the desirability of accepting articles as evidence of tenurability, and a few departments are receptive to these arguments, but they remain a minority. The best way to avoid this predicament is to choose a dissertation topic that is adequate to the demands that book publication will impose.

3

TURNING YOUR DISSERTATION
RIGHTSIDE OUT

Scott Norton

Most academic authors seem to assume that their subjects will interest only other specialists in their fields. Yet, as an editor who has worked on books in areas ranging from medieval Japanese literature to the political applications of game theory, I rarely encounter a manuscript that does not yield an insight I find personally illuminating. True, those nuggets are sometimes buried on page 314—but they are there. The trick is to excavate those rough gems and place them in the discursive foreground, to recast the book in such a way as to appeal not only to a broader array of scholars but maybe even to that elusive audience of intelligent lay readers.

Some scholars are excellent researchers or innovative thinkers who simply lack writing skills. But many academic authors have the requisite skills as well as research subjects of significant appeal, yet their efforts are hampered by their reliance on scholarly style and format. In the next chapter, I'll offer ways to address matters of style and tone; in this chapter I want to focus on the greatest challenge facing the aspiring "crossover" author—revision of organizational structure. This almost always includes shifting the focus of the discourse to a revised central thesis and restructuring the table of contents.

What follows is a fictional case study that exhibits most of the organizational challenges I've encountered. Your manuscript will almost certainly not require all these interventions. Nor will your publisher likely be able to offer you the degree of editorial involvement that I describe: such "developmental editing" is expensive and rarely figures into the economics of first books for new authors. But reviewing your text in the light of each of these steps should be a useful exercise in vetting its structure for audience appeal. A convenient checklist appears at the end of the chapter.

In most cases, revising a dissertation for publication involves turning its structure inside out. Theory shifts from foreground to background and content from background to foreground. A line of conceptual discourse recedes and a narrative line emerges. Actually, I think of the process as turning the organizational structure rightside out—the dissertation arrives inside out in the first place. I'm not making a value judgment here. If you look at an intricately patterned sock that has been turned inside out, what do you see? All the knots and stitches that hold it together. This view is of great interest to other makers of socks but not to the sock's wearer. Both views are useful, but to different groups. Similarly, dissertations tend to express their theoretical underpinnings prominently while assuming that the reader knows the pattern— the content—that lies beneath.

Turning a dissertation inside out is a scary proposition. Most scholars worry that the originality of their research and thought

will become camouflaged under operatic costumes and scenery—
they fret that their discourse will be "dumbed down." Indeed, this
danger is real. Yet successful scholarly books walk that narrow line
between theoretical discourse and traditional narrative. The challenge is no small one, but it is the challenge that faces all academic
authors today.

Without further ado, let's turn to the case of Professor Peter
Wade, who has written a manuscript provisionally entitled *Contested Origins: The Life of Brother Loukas of Athos.* Forgive the pre-
posterous central conceit, but I want to make sure that my example does not breach confidentiality by resembling any book
I've actually worked on.

ASSESSING MARKET GOALS

For three summers, graduate student Peter Wade labored in the
main library at Mount Athos, the famous theocratic republic of
Orthodox monks. Through a fluke of kinship, he has been given
unparalleled access to this cache of treasures and has made a discovery that caused quite a stir at a recent annual convention of
historians of science. His revelation: that a brilliant monk named
Loukas, studying the unique flora and fauna that thrive on the
Halkidiki Peninsula—at the easternmost promontory of which
Mount Athos is situated—arrived at scientifically accurate theo-
ries of heredity and evolution decades before Charles Darwin and
Gregor Mendel.

Drew Hanson—an acquisitions editor at the University of
California Press—hears Wade's presentation and approaches the
dais afterward. Wade's dissertation has already been completed
and accepted by his committee, and editors from Yale and Har-

vard are courting him with book deals. The next morning, Wade and Drew meet for breakfast and commiserate over the conundrum facing the first-book author in twenty-first-century scholarship. On the one hand, Wade sees Brother Loukas as a case study that challenges the hegemony of Western culture over the history of science in the late premodern era—he wants to "take on the establishment" and believes that the book, properly revised, could get reviewed nationally in the media. On the other hand, he'd like to find a tenure-track job within that same establishment, and the rigors through which his dissertation committee just recently put him have made him think twice about his brasher aspirations.

Drew observes that undermining Western bias in the history of modern science sounds like a career-long battle, in which the Brother Loukas story may be but the first volley. Drew draws three concentric rings representing three possible audiences that Wade might reach with this first book.

The inmost circle—historians of science, perhaps fifteen hundred worldwide—could be reached without much revision. The book would get good coverage in the relevant scholarly journals. Wade would be surest of his tenure prospects and could undertake future research projects with greater intellectual freedom. In University of California Press parlance, the result would be a *special interest* title.

The middle circle extends the narrative's appeal to scholars in related disciplines—biologists, medical specialists, scholars of Byzantine culture, and so on—plus a smattering of educated lay readers. To reach this audience of three to five thousand, Wade would make his book more accessible, most likely a straight intellectual biography. The book would be reviewed widely, and the resulting press could work for or against Wade's tenure aspirations, depending on the politics of his department. At California, we'd call this a *midlist* title.

The outermost circle would embrace the segment of the educated general public interested in the topic, as many as ten or twelve thousand readers. Wade would need to imbue the biographical narrative with vivid character descriptions, a compelling plot, and colorful evocations of the subject's cultural milieu. This ambitious rewrite might expose Wade to negative comments by conservative reviewers in the specialized journals, but it might also open many doors. UC Press would get fully behind the book as one of its frontlist *trade* titles.

A few weeks later, Wade decides he'd like to attempt a revision of the manuscript that shoots for the middle ring, the midlist plan. He'd be inclined to sign a contract with California if—all other terms being equal—he could count on some strong guidance during revision. Drew is pretty sure he can wangle a grant from the Greek Ministry of Cultural Affairs for Wade's book, so he decides to budget for developmental editing despite the book's modest market expectations. That's where I come in.

SHIFTING FOCUS

A quick look at the table of contents discloses that the manuscript will require a complete change of focus (see figure 3.1). The organizational structure is sound, but it is built on a central thesis that emphasizes the scholarly import of the author's research. Put another way, the discourse tells a story, but it is the story of the author's journey of intellectual discovery, not the story of Brother Loukas's life. The sock is inside out. How can I

Figure 3.1 *The Unedited Table of Contents*

Contested Origins: The Life of Brother Loukas of Athos

Introduction: The Road to Lavra

PART I. CONTESTED SOURCES

1. "The Library Is a Shambles": Reconstructing the Early Field Notes
2. In Search of the Yannina Syllabi, 1764–68

PART II. "ON THIS WINDY PROMONTORY": CONTESTED INFERENCES

3. Toward a Binary Theory of Heredity
4. Toward a Selective-Adaptation Theory of Evolution
5. "Against Lamarckism" (1790)

PART III. CONTESTED RESULTS

6. Debated Spirits, Spirited Debates: The Firestorm around "The Electrical Properties of Heredity" (1804)

PART IV. CONTESTED INFLUENCES

7. Galvanism or Loukism? The Cultural Politics of Scientific History
8. Darwin and "That Greek Holy Man": A Study in Denial
9. "God Is in the Details": The Parallel Careers of Mendel and Loukas

Conclusion: Avenues of Further Study

---

tell this by looking at a contents page? All the telltale signs are there. The chapters are few and long; the chapter titles emphasize scholarly sources and theories; dates are included for landmark primary sources; quotations are used intermittently as part and chapter titles. Particularly unfortunate is the liberal use of the word *contested* in the book and chapter titles: this word, besides being criminally overemployed, signals the author's intention to represent multiple sides of a debate without weighing in decisively himself.

CREATING A CONTENT SUMMARY

The introduction begins nicely enough with Wade embarking on his third annual pilgrimage, on a bus careening along the narrow, cliff-hugging road to the thousand-year-old Great Lavra monastery. But then the author lapses into a twenty-page reverie about a journal page he discovered during his previous visit; during this extended flashback, he reviews a trail of archival evidence that supports an early date for the journal page. To Wade's colleagues, the implications would be clear and dramatically exciting: the early diary entry shows a youthful Loukas already contemplating key hereditary issues. But to me, the connection and its import are far from apparent—and Wade doesn't make the link explicit until page 79, at the end of an overlong first chapter in which he details his methodology for dating the monk's vast store of papers.

As I skim the entire manuscript, information continues to bombard me in a sequence that is not intuitive to my nonspecialist brain, though historians of science would undoubtedly see its logic. By the last page I'm able to piece together a summary of the subject's biographical and intellectual highlights:

> Brother Loukas (1751–1819), dean of the Athonite Academy, Greek Orthodox monk and groundbreaking biologist. Sometimes called "the Byzantine Mendel" because of superficial similarities with the later Austrian monk-scientist.
>
> Born Dimitri Jaki to a family of goatherds in Zagoria. At age twelve, he collected a unique species of orchid in a local ravine. His specimen, sent to the regional capital of Yannina,

won him a scholarship there. At the university in this Muslim-influenced city (1764–68), he studied the new classification system of Carl Linnaeus, Ben Franklin's famous treatises on electricity (1748–52), and the rudiments of medicine. After a scandal involving a dalliance with the daughter of a muezzin, Dimitri was sent to Mount Athos (1769) to teach in the Athonite Academy, where he served as instructor in botany and assistant to the barber-surgeon.

As Brother Loukas, he remained in Athos most of his life, collecting botanical specimens and conducting medical experiments. He became the academy's chief physician in 1778 and its dean in 1786. In 1809, invited to lecture at Yannina, Loukas met the young English poet Lord Byron. He returned to Athos in 1814; two years after his death there of old age, revolutionaries fighting the Greek War of Independence ransacked the libraries of Athos, scattering his papers.

Loukas's observations of static in human hair gave rise to his first experiments with galvanism, the technique eventually named after Luigi Galvani (1737–98), whose discovery of so-called animal electricity (1791) Loukas anticipated by two decades. He theorized that all living creatures have souls made up of electrical energy, then set about proving his idea by running electrical currents through the nerves of dead frogs and roosters and amputated human limbs. Using this erroneous premise, he correctly identified two principles governing the evolution of species: the binary nature of heredity and the process of selective adaptation. These discoveries anticipated the work of Charles Darwin (1809–82) and Gregor Mendel (1822–84) by half a century.

In Loukas's theory of heredity, particles of positively or negatively charged matter in the tissues of parents determine the traits inherited by offspring, much as genes are known to function today. Loukas had to account for the fact that, in his electrical tests, a charge shared by two objects would cause them to repel each other, whereas in his hereditary experiments a trait shared by both parents "attracted" that trait to the offspring. He decided that an individual trait, such as brown hair, could be positively charged in one parent and negatively charged in the other, thus causing brown hair in the offspring; if the trait was positively or negatively charged in both parents, the trait would be suppressed. The mathematical outcomes were remarkably prescient of Mendel's results with pea plants decades later.

But Loukas's greatest accomplishment was to link the heredity mechanism to the evolutionary process. The deep canyons of his native region and the stark promontories of the Athos peninsula created insular effects on speciation not unlike those later encountered by Darwin in the Galapagos. Populations of wildflowers, reptiles, and rodents separated by only a few kilometers, but cut off from each other by steep cliffs, evolved over time into distinctive species because of two factors: (1) the different mathematical outcomes of heredity; and (2) adaptive responses to the differences in local conditions such as direct light, aridity, and soil content.

Loukas's published papers on both discoveries received widespread attention in the late eighteenth century, but by the middle of the nineteenth century his work was all but forgotten. Cloaking his theories in the language of spirit—that is, equating electrical charges with animating spirit—allowed him to avoid charges of blasphemy in his religious community but ultimately prejudiced scientific rationalists against him.

I realize that Wade's original organizational strategy is indeed sound for an audience of specialists: he has traced the development of Loukas's key concepts, placing them in the larger context of the history of biological studies, taking care to distinguish valid observations from religious cant, and subordinating biographical details—in fact, often burying them in footnotes. Once unraveled, the story he tells is fascinating. It is worth the effort needed to turn it into a book.

DISTINGUISHING BETWEEN THESES AND SUBJECTS

The manuscript identifies many themes explicitly, but more often Wade presents undigested content as though its thematic implications were self-evident. The next step is to sift through the tremendous amount of material he's amassed and to distinguish theses from raw subject matter.

On a legal pad, I write headings for two columns, "Subjects" and "Possible Theses." In the first column, I note each subject I encounter, along with its page number; in the second, I expand those subjects into statements that make a leap of conceptual relevance for the reader (see figure 3.2). Wade's peers can be expected to make these leaps without his spelling them out, but the other readers we are hoping to reach will require help.

DISTINGUISHING BETWEEN THESES AND THEORETICAL FRAMEWORKS

After the first long chapter, the themes multiply quickly. The author has lived with the ghost of Loukas so long that he has considered the monk's life from every point of view—his faith, his sexuality, his medical practice—and the text is replete with fascinating insights, albeit arranged in nonlinear fashion. At one point, for example, Wade links the thousand-year-old banishment from the Athos peninsula of all things female—women, hens, milk, sows—to Loukas's view of gender. But his perspective on gender

Figure 3.2 *Identifying Possible Theses*

Subjects	Possible Theses
L.'s field notes on endemic rodents, reptiles, and wildflowers	L.'s field notes show the beginnings of an understanding of adaptive selection in evolution.
L.'s introduction to Orthodox mysticism	L.'s introduction to Orthodox mysticism laid the groundwork for a dynamic conception of the human soul that L. would later link to electricity.
L. waits table during Ottoman envoy's visit	Called on to serve at table during the meals taken by the abbot and an envoy from the Ottoman Empire, L. gained insight into political tensions that would shape his career.

is unclear, and the topic isn't broached again. Though a trade publisher might be satisfied with a straightforward narrative of Loukas's life, I know the Press will want to retain this deeper critical thinking.

I return to my list, breaking it into three columns instead of two. First, I make additions to the subject column; next I make parallel entries in a new column, headed "Theoretical Frameworks"; and then I attempt the expansive leaps to thesis statements that Wade seems to be implying (see figure 3.3). Of the dozen possible theses I've identified, some hold more promise than others. I keep adding to the list without attempting to edit it, treating this pass through the manuscript as a brainstorming exercise. All the while, I am looking for a single thesis large enough to embrace most, if not all, of the others.

Figure 3.3 *Identifying More Possible Theses*

Subjects	Theoretical Frameworks	Possible Theses
L.'s field notes on endemic rodents, reptiles, and wildflowers	Science	L.'s field notes show the beginnings of an understanding of adaptive selection in evolution.
L.'s introduction to Orthodox mysticism	Religion	L.'s introduction to Orthodox mysticism laid the groundwork for a dynamic conception of the human soul that L. would later link to electricity.
L. waits table during Ottoman envoy's visit	Politics	Called on to serve at table during the meals taken by the abbot and an envoy from the Ottoman empire, L. gained insight into political tensions that would shape his career
L.'s tendency to skip liturgical offices	Religion	L.'s absenteeism from daily liturgical offices showed a rebellious streak that presaged his willingness to challenge conventional theories of biology.
Proscription against females at Athos	Gender theory	Removal of females from his daily life heightened L.'s awareness of the roles of the sexes in human society and contributed to his thinking about inherited characteristics.
Tension in L.'s relationship with barber-physician	Society	Tension in L.'s relationship with the community's barber-physician was an an early indication of L.'s departure from standard medical philosophy.

CHOOSING A MAIN THESIS

By the time I reach the last page, I've identified more than thirty concepts that could conceivably serve as the main thesis. I mull over the list a while, eliminating those not broad enough to encompass most of Wade's material, and end up with six possibilities.

Faith: Orthodox mysticism provided L. with a conceptual framework within which to explore electricity as the physical link between the spirit and human worlds.

Society: The cloister gave L. a protected environment in which to experiment without interference from other Greek scholars or society at large.

Gender: L.'s thwarted love life, along with his skewed experience of gender on the Athos peninsula, ironically provided key insights into the role of reproduction in evolution.

Romanticism: L.'s lifelong fascination with Romantic literature informed his image of himself as a genius and emboldened him to challenge conventional religious and scientific thought.

Politics: Anti-imperialist sentiment in his native Zagoria bolstered L.'s resolve to conceptualize beyond the strictures of established doctrine, whether religious or scientific.

Rationalism: L.'s hardscrabble childhood disposed him toward the tenets of rationalism at the university, which in turn inspired his scientific approach toward mysticism.

These are promising options, but choosing among them would bind the narrative to a single theoretical framework. Is there a common thread running through the six choices that would allow them all to find expression? Late in his manuscript, Wade observes that when Loukas created his theory of heredity by inverting the properties of electricity, he showed a resourceful use of paradox that characterized his entire life. He had already turned a childhood of abject rural poverty into a season of intellectual discovery; an adolescent scandal into a good career move; a religious vocation into a scientific one. Finally, I have found a formulation that seems to work:

> Paradox: L.'s theory of heredity was an extension of his deeply held personal belief that all of life is characterized by paradox, namely, the dynamic coexistence of opposing forces.

Whether Wade will buy this as his main thesis is somewhat beside the point. My purpose in drafting this main thesis is not to put words into the author's mouth but to model the process by which he might arrive at his own workable thesis.

CREATING A WORKING TITLE

Before I can make a revision proposal to the author, I need to generate at least one outline that will demonstrate how his vast store of material might be reorganized without dictating how the text must ultimately be arranged. The best outline will arise out of creative tension between my push for organization and the author's championing of the lively essence of his material.

But before I begin outlining, I want to choose a suitable working title. My goal is not to find the Perfect Title at this early stage but rather to determine what emphasis the title will impart so that the chapter titles I draft will follow logically. I try *The Darwin of*

Byzantium, The Rope Ladder, The Noah Mosaic, and *The Slow Light-ning of the Soul,* and to each I append the same subtitle, *How a Greek Monk Anticipated the Theory of Evolution.*

The first choice plays up the surprise of an Eastern contribution to innovations normally perceived as "Western." The second refers to the rope ladder by which monks ascended to the cliffside hermitages at Athos, an image that Loukas used to explain the evolution of species from lower taxa to higher. The third draws on another image from Athos: the mosaic of Noah's ark in the Great Lavra sanctuary, which Loukas frequently contemplated as he attempted to put together the pieces of the evolution story. The fourth quotes a line from Loukas's diary to link his electrical experiments on severed limbs with the creative spirit that he considered the guiding force of evolution. I decide on this option because it is dramatic, spiritual, and reflective of Loukas's unique scientific approach.

BRAINSTORMING OUTLINES

Most scholarly works combine two basic narrative strategies: chronological development and thematic development. Telling a story in straightforward motion through time—with the occasional flashback or flashforward—is the safest and often the most effective route toward a compelling scholarly midlist trade book. But because scholarship traffics in ideas, the "story" of a university press book is often the development of a concept or theory. The choice becomes a matter of proportion: how much narrative versus how much discourse. By mapping chronological milestones against the main conceptual themes I've identified (faith, society, gender, politics, paradox), then reversing that strategy, I should be able to clarify the range of organizational options for Wade's book (see figure 3.4).

Romanticism and rationalism do not rise to the level of importance that would justify devoting whole chapters to them, so I leave those themes out of my schema. The resulting outlines, while admittedly mechanical, are illustrative. Option 1 would tell Loukas's life story in the manner of a novel whose omniscient narrator returns to a handful of main themes at regular intervals. The challenge would be to ensure that the themes were linked explicitly enough that their arguments would cohere when retraced through the text; the danger would be a tendency to repeat material to remind the reader of the context for each new theoretical development. Option 2 would make linking the thematic developments much easier, and scholars in gender studies, religious studies, history of science, and related fields would be more inclined to reference these chapters, perhaps assigning the book as supplemental reading in their classes. But the danger would be loss of narrative momentum—the reader would traverse the milestones of Loukas's life four times over, and it would be tricky to ensure that subsequent traverses were as interesting as the first.

CHOOSING AND FINE-TUNING AN OUTLINE

I send Wade these examples as possible bases for a thesis statement and outline of his own device. Wade thinks the paradox thesis is "exactly right" and likes many of my proposed chapters in outline Option 1. He notes, however, that my outlines emphasize contextual, interpretive factors at the expense of Loukas's actual scientific experiments and discoveries: "Where is the moment when L. discovers his unique orchid species? Where is the dra-

Figure 3.4 *Two Possible Outlines*

The Slow Lightning of the Soul: How a Greek Monk Anticipated the Theory of Evolution

Option 1

PART I. THE GOATHERD BOY

1. A Gun in the Cradle (faith)
2. The Village *Plaka* (society)
3. A Broken Rosary (gender)
4. Rebel Causes, Rebel Effects (politics)
5. Farewell to Zagoria (paradox)

PART II. THE URBANE STUDENT

6. Bedtime Prayers (faith)
7. Easter in a Strange Land (society)
8. The Muezzin's Daughter (gender)
9. Café Banter (politics)
10. Into God's Custody (paradox)

PART III. THE NOVICE

11. The Soul of Hair (faith)
12. On Cloistered Grounds (society)
13. Wild Females (gender)
14. The Envoy's Visit (politics)
15. Solemn Vows (paradox)

PART IV. THE DEAN

16. Lightning Strikes Twice (faith)
17. Brushes with Fame (society)
18. Letters from an Empress (gender)
19. Signs of Unrest (politics)
20. Second Thoughts (paradox)

PART V. THE HERMIT

21. Jubilee (faith)
22. Return to Yannina (society)
23. Unveilings (gender)
24. A Byronic Encounter (politics)
25. Doxology (paradox)

Figure 3.4 *(continued)*

Option 2

PART I. DIVINE INSPIRATIONS (FAITH)

1. A Gun in the Cradle
2. Bedtime Prayers
3. The Soul of Hair
4. Lightning Strikes Twice
5. Jubilee

PART II. SOCIAL GRACES (SOCIETY)

6. The Village *Plaka*
7. Easter in a Strange Land
8. On Cloistered Grounds
9. Brushes with Fame
10. Return to Yannina

PART III. THE FEMININE PRINCIPLE (GENDER)

11. A Broken Rosary
12. The Muezzin's Daughter
13. Wild Females
14. Letters from an Empress
15. Unveilings

PART IV. INSURGENCIES (POLITICS)

16. Rebel Causes, Rebel Effects
17. Café Banter
18. The Envoy's Visit
19. Signs of Unrest
20. A Byronic Encounter

PART V. THE ATTRACTION OF OPPOSITES (PARADOX)

21. Farewell to Zagoria
22. Into God's Custody
23. Solemn Vows
24. Second Thoughts
25. Doxology

matic moment when he hooks up iron and copper electrodes to the severed limb of a fellow monk?" He's right, of course—in this respect, I've missed the forest for the trees.

Wade also has problems with the elevated status of the gender theme. He would like to downplay the scandal with the young woman in Yannina, as well as the importance of the "antifemale" culture of the Athonite enclave. Although I disagree, Wade seems adamant on this point, most likely in deference to the feelings of monks whom he has gotten to know personally on his summers in Athos. So, after several rounds of e-mail, we settle on a revised version of outline Option 1 that demotes the gender theme and promotes a new theme labeled "science" (see figure 3.5). To test the validity of "science" as a theme, I ask him to come up with a thesis statement, and he does:

> Science: From an early age, L. demonstrated an appetite for scientific knowledge that exposed him to the latest discoveries and theories in Western thought—ideas that often contrasted starkly with the values held by his Orthodox culture.

This thesis works beautifully; it amalgamates and extends the themes of Romanticism and rationalism. Now the science chapters provide the climax for each part in the narrative, with each paradox chapter serving as dénouement.

RESPONDING TO SCHOLARLY REVIEWS

Meanwhile, Drew has sent two copies of the manuscript to experts in Wade's field. Every book published by the Press must have letters showing that two peers support its publication.

Figure 3.5 *The Chosen Outline, First Revision*

The Slow Lightning of the Soul: How a Greek Monk Anticipated the Theory of Evolution

PART I. THE GOATHERD BOY

1. A Gun in the Cradle (faith)
2. The Village *Plaka* (society)
3. Rebel Causes, Rebel Effects (politics)
4. A Prize Orchid (science)
5. Farewell to Zagoria (paradox)

PART II. THE URBANE STUDENT

6. Bedtime Prayers (faith)
7. Easter in a Strange Land (society)
8. Café Banter (politics)
9. Between Iron and Copper (science)
10. Into God's Custody (paradox)

PART III. THE NOVICE

11. The Soul of Hair (faith)
12. On Cloistered Grounds (society)
13. The Envoy's Visit (politics)
14. An Amputation (science)
15. Solemn Vows (paradox)

PART IV. THE DEAN

16. Lightning Strikes Twice (faith)
17. Brushes with Fame (society)
18. Signs of Unrest (politics)
19. Current Attractions (science)
20. Second Thoughts (paradox)

PART V. THE HERMIT

21. Jubilee (faith)
22. Return to Yannina (society)
23. A Byronic Encounter (politics)
24. Obscurity Regained (science)
25. Doxology (paradox)

Reader #1 supports publication enthusiastically, calling the manuscript "an important work of original research on a long-neglected subject with ramifications for the study of the history of science across the East-West cultural divide." She finds the text well organized, the thesis cogently argued, and the documentation thorough. Her one concern is Wade's "neglect of the gender issue."

Reader #2 also supports publication, but with more qualms. He disagrees with Reader #1 about the adequacy of the scholarship—in his opinion, Wade's remarkable access to primary sources has led him to overlook secondary sources that have a bearing on the theme of Occidentalist bias in the historiography of science. He recommends adding text discussions of the relevance of the work of J. on Marco Polo, K. on Mayan mathematics, and L. on an obscure Korean woman, contemporaneous with Loukas, who served as imperial zookeeper. Reader #2 requests that his name be withheld from the report, but Wade quickly discerns that his identity is none other than L.

Press policy requires that Wade respond to the reports with a memo detailing which recommendations he will implement and which he rejects, and on what grounds. Wade explains that his omission of the works cited by Reader #2 was not accidental but derived from his sense that citing the work of other non-Occidental scientists was irrelevant. Loukas would not have known of the Mayan or Korean discoveries, and his theories did not rely on any discoveries made by Marco Polo. The revisions promised are limited to footnotes and to an epilogue that places Loukas in the larger context of overlooked non-Occidental scientific innovators. Wade also promises to add a few paragraphs on the application of gender theory to Loukas's scientific views, but he continues to resist elevating gender to the status of a recurring theme.

ADDING CHAPTER THESES

The next step is to develop a thesis for each chapter. Impatient to begin the rewrite proper, Wade asks whether we can't skip this step, but I assure him that taking time now to bring each chapter into conceptual focus will make rewriting much easier down the road. For the first chapter, he sends me the following:

1. A Gun in the Cradle (faith)

   Young L. grows up in a mountain community rife with feuds, among eight brothers who mock his love of God and nature.

This statement seems more like plot summary than theme. What, I ask, is the relevance of this event to the book's main thesis? After several tries, he succeeds in mapping out true theses for all of part I:

1. A Gun in the Cradle (faith)

   Early on, as a sensitive nature lover among the feuding herdsmen of his native village, L. develops the faith in God's continuing acts of creativity that will eventually empower him to make his great discoveries.

2. The Village *Plaka* (society)

   L.'s early years, divided between the village square and the local gorges, display the combination of solitude and intensely communal life that will characterize his adult life.

3. Rebel Causes, Rebel Effects (politics)

   L.'s lifelong avoidance of political controversy is rooted in the futility he saw in a political battle that erupted in his village during his childhood.

4. A Prize Orchid (science)

   The young L.'s precocious discovery of a new species of orchid demonstrates an intuitive awareness of the as-yet-undiscovered principle of variation in evolutionary biology.

5. Farewell to Zagoria (paradox)

   Though L. feels he is "escaping" the mountains when he receives a scholarship to cosmopolitan Yannina, he carries with him values, and a love of nature, that will remain with him for life.

Over the course of a week, the author and I trade e-mails until all twenty-five chapters have theses.

WEIGHTING CHAPTERS EQUALLY

The next labor-intensive task in our process is to figure out what goes into each chapter. I earmark passages in the manuscript for their new chapters, noting the length of each and assigning it a working subhead. The narrative chunks are easy to situate; the conceptual ones will need to be positioned by Wade himself, but I place them tentatively so I can take stock of how the chapters are shaping up. It becomes apparent that some are too long and others too short. In Part I, for instance, Chapters 1, 4, and 5 average twenty pages but Chapters 2 and 3 average ten pages. The author and I agree that this imbalance is because the two chapters are in fact related, both being about early social influences on Loukas's character and thought, so we agree to combine the two chapters. We continue through the outline, combining short chapters and breaking up long ones, until we arrive at a set of chapters evenly sized at between fifteen and twenty-five pages apiece. The resulting outline is much less formulaic than my drafts and much more satisfying.

CREATING TRANSITIONS

It's time to get down to editing. I begin working my way through the chapters, finalizing the order of the passages we've earmarked for each and writing transitions between them.

The greatest challenge at this stage is managing the openings and closings of each chapter. Some existing passages function as natural introductions and conclusions, but often there is no language in the text that can serve these purposes clearly and succinctly. I remodel our chapter thesis statements into introductory sentences, making use of whatever colorful details I can find in neighboring passages. For instance, I suggest beginning the new Chapter 3, "A Prize Orchid," with a detail that restates the sociopolitical thesis of the new Chapter 2 (which combines the former Chapters 2 and 3) while introducing the new scientific thesis:

> Often, to escape the shouting matches outside the taverna in his village's *plaka*—arguments that grew louder and more tense as he entered his twelfth year—Loukas would take a steep path into one of the local gorges, clambering nimbly as a goat. It was on one of these long walks that he first noticed the tiny orchid that would soon bear his name.

Concluding statements vary more widely. Some, as in Chapter 3, restate the present thesis while foreshadowing the next:

> Loukas's orchid afforded him a glimpse into his future—and the future of science. The verification of his identification by the academy in Athens marked the end of his childhood and the first step toward leaving his rugged Zagoria.

Other chapters end, not with explicit summation, but with a plot development, a "cliff-hanger," that entices the reader to find out "what happens next." This venerable device can be overused (read any Anne Rice novel), but it is a useful tool in the story-teller's kit.

INTEGRATING NARRATIVE AND THEORY

I send Wade each of the five parts as it's completed to give him an opportunity to review the integration of narrative material with scholarly theory. For instance, I feel we should introduce Loukas's concept of the electrical soul in the first chapter, since Loukas's diary portrays his childhood as the point at which he first felt the mystical infilling that would inspire his work. But Wade argues that Loukas was mythologizing his past with the benefit of hind-sight and that mysticism was an unlikely element of early child-hood in the rough, feud-torn mountains of Zagoria. We agree to foreshadow the mysticism in the first chapter but to defer a de-tailed discussion of the concept to a later chapter in which a ma-ture Loukas fully explicates his theory of the marriage of spirit and body via electricity.

We also spar a bit about the length of conceptual passages. Wade feels that the reader will be better served if complex topics are discussed in self-contained mini-discourses. Thus, in the chapter entitled "The Soul of Hair," Loukas the barber's assistant, having recently devoured Benjamin Franklin's famous treatise on electricity, takes up the broom to sweep his brothers' fallen locks of hair and decides that their lifelike movements, caused by static electricity, must be evidence of the physical nature of the soul re-siding in all animate things. At this pivotal moment, Wade wishes to insert five pages describing the career of Luigi Galvani, discoverer of "animal electricity" and namesake of the process of galvanism. I'm afraid keeping this lengthy "aside" intact will make the reader impatient to resume Loukas's story. We agree to allow three main theoretical detours, and to situate them all in chapters that focus on the theme of science.

Aside from these crucial mini-treatises, Wade and I agree to dissolve all blocks of conceptual discourse thoroughly into the narrative. In a few places, Loukas breaks into long interior monologues as though he were an Umberto Eco character, but this is the best we can do: editing, like so many other joint human endeavors, is the art of compromise.

DRAWING CONCLUSIONS, THEN PLACING THEM

The most challenging aspect of managing the integration of scholarly discourse and narrative is to draw proper conclusions and place them to advantage. Many scholars who spend years in the trenches of research become reluctant to draw conclusions from their findings: acutely aware that a late discovery can shed new light on a theory, completely revising it, they err on the side of letting others interpret their data for them. Wade is a member of this camp of scholarly conservatives, but his saving grace is a deep conviction regarding the importance of his subject. No matter how hard he tries, he cannot camouflage his belief that Brother Loukas was a major thinker whose work influenced the course of Western science and culture. His discourse is underpinned by three strong conclusions, each of which we place in the text after much strategizing.

Wade's first strong conclusion is that Loukas's theory of heredity greatly resembles the one proven by that other monk, Gregor Mendel, nearly a century later. Given that Wade has found no evidence that Mendel knew Loukas's work, and that Mendel solved the problem via statistical probability—that is, by a method that was the antithesis of Loukas's metaphysics—this conclusion alone would not warrant a claim for Loukas's vaunted place in the history of science.

Wade's second remarkable conclusion is that Loukas may have directly influenced the thought of Charles Darwin. Darwin spoke disparagingly of the "Greek holy man," and the metaphysical language in which Loukas expressed his theories was often used to discredit him. Nevertheless, Loukas's careful study of variation among species, first in the Zagorian gorges and later on the Athonite peninsula—both with isolating physical landscapes much like Darwin's Galapagos—predates by decades the work of Darwin's acknowledged forebear, Thomas Malthus. Field notes discovered by Wade in the Lavra archives support the claim.

Wade's third and most important conclusion is that Loukas was the first to intuit a connection between the heredity mechanism and the process of evolution. The discoveries of Darwin and Mendel were made without reference to each other. Darwin's camp labored under the misconception of Lamarck's theory of "acquired characteristics," which held that adult organisms could pass on new characteristics to their offspring by altering their behavior. This fallacy, which greatly slowed the progress of evolutionary theory, had been disproven by Loukas as early as 1790.

We settle on a plan to drop the Darwin bomb in "Lightning Strikes Twice," where Loukas's publication of his theory generates an explosion of controversy similar to that which later met *The Origin of Species*. The Mendel connection will be remarked on in "Between Copper and Iron," since it was during those early days of experimentation that Loukas first hit on his idea of hereditary binarism. And the third, synthetic revelation will be unveiled in "Obscurity Regained," as Loukas sinks into old age and neglect by the new faculty of the Athonite Academy.

CUTTING FOR LENGTH

Our acquisitions editor, Drew, discovers the revised manuscript is 15 percent longer than he's budgeted for. Readers of historical biographies don't mind fat tomes, but Drew is concerned that we'll lose our course market if the book is over 250 pages. Wade and I set out to whittle the text down to size. We ask ourselves two questions: (1) Are any passages entirely expendable? (2) Are any passages characterized by multiple examples when one will do?

We briefly consider omitting the encounter with Lord Byron but, realizing that this historical gossip will catch the eye of prospective reviewers, we leave the chapter in. Instead, we find places where we can eliminate multiple examples: one trip to the orchid gorge instead of three, one tryst with the muezzin's daughter instead of four, one attempt at electrical reanimation of a severed limb. In each case, we choose the most interesting of the examples, develop it into a vivid scene, and then succinctly summarize the other examples. We do our best to cut equal amounts from most chapters to preserve the hard-won balance among them.

REPEATING SUCCESS

When released for publication, *The Slow Lightning of the Soul* gets full-page treatment in the *New York Times Book Review*. The reviewer blasts Wade's timid handling of Loukas's gender views but otherwise finds the book "a fascinating account of a neglected giant in the history of science." The first printing of five thousand copies sells out in six months.

Drew tells me that Wade has signed another contract with the Press, for a book whose revelations will garner as least as much attention as those in *Slow Lightning.* On his fourth summer in the Lavra archives, Wade discovered evidence that a vision recorded in Loukas's journal, and transmitted orally by Lord Byron himself, formed the basis for Mary Shelley's famous gothic tale of Dr. Frankenstein. Wade e-mails me his thesis and outline before he writes the text, and I can see that he's absorbed the lessons he learned in our first collaboration. He's steered clear of the pitfall of repeating material already covered in the published book, and his decision to focus equally on the lives of Loukas, Byron, and Shelley during the single year of 1816 bodes well for a brisk read. This time, he's shooting for the brass ring—a bona fide trade readership.

"You don't need me anymore," I reply with mock wistfulness. I pull up a copy of the memo I first sent him and list the steps for him so that he can be sure to follow them in his new venture:

- Assessing market goals
- Shifting focus
- Creating a content summary
- Distinguishing between theses and subjects
- Distinguishing between theses and theoretical frameworks
- Choosing a main thesis
- Creating a working title

- Brainstorming outlines
- Choosing and fine-tuning an outline
- Responding to scholarly reviews
- Adding chapter theses
- Weighting chapters equally
- Creating transitions
- Integrating narrative and theory
- Drawing conclusions, then placing them
- Cutting for length

For kicks, I pull out my complimentary copy of *Slow Lightning* and compare the outline I first proposed with the contents page of the printed version. The deviations are more numerous than I remembered, and for a moment I'm appalled at the number of misconceptions implicit in my initial plan. But I remind myself that my purpose was to prompt Wade to find solutions to his own problems, not to provide them for him. The final text is all his.

4

BRINGING YOUR OWN VOICE TO THE TABLE

Scott Norton

One of the more memorable tables I've eaten at was an unhinged door laid flat and held up by sawhorses. It had white linen thrown over it and was situated at the end of a full-sized bed in a railroad apartment crammed with books and cat hair. Around this table four nights a week would gather the intelligentsia and not-so-intelligentsia of the Princeton area; one evening I'd find myself rubbing elbows with an astrophysicist and a novelist, the next with an ancient ballerina and a manic socialite. The host was a fiery Irish poet from Boston, a lank fussy man in his fifties, with salt-and-pepper hair and exactly half his mustache turned white. He typed up legal documents for a meager living and supplemented his income by serving a three-course meal for five dollars (a bargain, even in the early 1980s) to guests who had heard about his Julia Child–inspired cooking via word of mouth. Eventually, he was featured under a pseudonym in *Talk about Town* and was promptly closed down by the Health Department.

What I remember most about that table was his voice. After

serving each course, he'd sit at the end of the door-table, watching us eat and moderating the conversation from a high stool. His voice ranged from basso profundo to screeches of delight, and his tone was by turns empathetic, mischievous, laudatory, teasing. He wittily summarized the résumé of each guest for the benefit of the others, then threw down a gauntlet to spark conversation—usually a political or religious topic, contra the etiquette mavens. If the conversation lulled, he upped the ante: "I'll see your local zoning problem and raise you the pope's misogyny." After dinner, select guests were invited to linger for a drink, and a second, rowdier gathering convened over the kitchen table. A hash pipe was lit, the astrophysicist told his dirtiest jokes, and hustlers and other parolees came and went until the wee hours.

While defending your dissertation, you may have found yourself the arbiter of conversation over a very different kind of table. Your committee was lined up on the far side of that table, with you centered opposite, pleading your case like a witness at a Senate hearing. The formality was palpable—the professionalism of your discipline required it. Your tone was sober and respectful, your responses were measured and conservative. Keen to show all you'd learned, you may have answered simple questions with long disquisitions—but this thoroughness of response was expected, even encouraged. And your writing naturally reflected this formality in its tone.

Now, with your dissertation successfully defended and ready to be revised for publication, it's time to shift its tenor. It's time for you to call those committee members around to your side of the table, to invite them home among relatives and friends, to loosen your tie and roll up your sleeves and laugh. How you celebrate— whether you serve braised lamb in your formal dining room or haul a six-pack onto the kitchen table—is up to you. You're the host. But whatever tack you take toward reworking your manuscript, remember that your committee members soldiered through your text because it was their job; in book form, your text will need to appeal to an audience that isn't captive. You'll need to convey your enthusiasm for your subject to an audience that may be as varied as the motley crew around my Princetonian host's two tables—and you'll have at your disposal all the wiles and tricks of style devised in the course of English literary history.

In the previous chapter, I presented a pretty comprehensive approach to revising the structure of your dissertation for publication. In doing so, I was drawing on rules of composition that have been in place for English since at least the late 1800s. There is no comprehensive set of rules for style, though attempts to provide such rules abound. In writing as in other forms of artistic endeavor, a successful style is a mystical blend of elements that are static when isolated. Strategies that work beautifully for one person will fall flat for another; one person's trademark is another person's tic.

In the pages that follow, we'll discuss how to identify your audience for stylistic purposes; consider five basic distinctions that govern stylistic choices; and review a glossary of stylistic elements that arise frequently in academic writing, with examples taken from about two dozen manuscripts I've edited over the past decade, some of them camouflaged in ways that render them historically inaccurate. (My apologies in advance to any reader who recognizes her own prose in these pages!) By making these choices with full awareness, and employing those elements that come most naturally, you should be able to bring your distinctive voice to the table.

IDENTIFYING YOUR AUDIENCE

When writing for broad dissemination, an author's tendency is to think in terms of entire disciplines, industries, even nations. In fact, your message may have that kind of reach, but if you're like most people, imagining your audience as a vast stadium crowd will be more intimidating than inspiring. Think of your audience as a group of roundtable discussants, with one individual whom you know personally representing each constituency you hope your book will reach.

Once you've completed this mental exercise, you will do two things with it. First, begin each writing session by reviewing the list—by reminding yourself to whom you are writing. Second, when you've finished your revisions, turn your imaginary audience into an actual one by asking each of the guests on your list to read your draft. Academic authors know to do this with their scholarship—an anthropologist writing a treatise on a community of Tibetan monks will naturally, almost reflexively, seek a reading from an expert in Eastern religions. But it is my experience that academic authors often aspire vaguely to reach an "intelligent lay public" without ever seeking reviews outside the academy.

Finally, among the members of your guest list be sure to include at least one enemy. Mentally surrounding yourself with enemies will turn your arguments harsh and shrill, but leavening a supportive discussion group with one or two formidable intellectual foes will sharpen your prose and guard against adopting a self-satisfied tone. If you insist on preaching to the choir, then your audience will not extend beyond the sanctuary.

CONTENT VERSUS STYLE

As you prepare to revise, you'll want to consider the balance of power between content and style as it relates to your own text. Of course, your content is already in place—the question is whether, and to what degree, you should alter your style. If your content is groundbreaking research and your book will serve as a primary source for others, you will not want to dress up your information in a style that distracts with its cleverness. If your content is synthetic scholarship and your book will serve as a secondary source for others, your style will need to be entertaining enough to draw, and keep, your readers' attention.

STYLE VERSUS FASHION

If you opt for a bolder style, ask yourself what elements are your trademarks. If those elements are of relatively recent vintage, incorporate them into your discourse judiciously—if you don't, you may become a fashion victim a few years down the road. (And it can take several years to get a manuscript published!) The identity politicians and cultural theorists of the last three decades are notorious cases: their (dis)courses be-came virtue-alley in/compre-HenSybil in their enthusiasm for rediscovering the roots of multisyllabic words and in their mistaking of bad puns for intellectual wit. Happily, that fad has largely passed.

As a first-time author, you will want to weigh the advantages and disadvantages of being in the avant-garde: the advance guard takes heavy casualties, and most of its heroes are forgotten by the time the major battles have passed. If you are truly a member of the avant-garde, press on—readers will, in small numbers, hear the originality of your voice and accept the eccentricities of your style as a kind of proof of your being "ahead of your time." Otherwise, before doing the intellectual equivalent of getting all your body parts tattooed and pierced, take a look at the hairstyle you're wearing in your junior high yearbook.

VOICE VERSUS VOICES

During my first creative writing workshop in college, when I read a poem of which I was particularly proud, the instructor complimented the dense rhythms and vivid language, then said with the merest smirk, "Been reading some Gerard Manley, have we?" I was astounded. I had in fact been immersed in an anthologized selection of Hopkins's work. I was so caught up in the discovery of this master's particular brand of beauty that I could not see my own experiments for what they were—shameless aping.

Since then I have seen this phenomenon at work in the writing of many young academic authors. I'm not always familiar with the mentors they're emulating, but the scent of mimicry is in the air. More often, these novices give themselves away by adopting the styles of more than one mentor, often juxtaposing styles so widely divergent they clang like pots and pans. When pressed to smooth out their tone, some of these postmoderns defend their style as bricolage, the scholarly equivalent of "sampling" in techno house music. But a good techno musician will tell you that sampling is harder than it sounds—in vinyl-scratching championships, the winner is whoever can surprise the audience with new aural moves. Mediocre sampling is worse than mediocre singing—it's the ultimate in derivative musical expression.

None of us can claim complete originality of thought or expression. We are all to some extent the sum of the various influences—interpersonal, cultural, economic, literary—that have impressed us. My poetry instructor didn't criticize me for writing in Hopkins mode; he encouraged me to mimic any poet whose work I admired but to acknowledge I was doing so and to work toward integrating the foreign mode into my natural manner.

This integration can be difficult to achieve when an exciting theory has just surfaced in your field. In the 1990s, many authors defended nonsensical constructions like "The author of the camera is dead" by saying that anyone who had read Barthes and Foucault would understand. Perhaps so, but anyone unfamiliar with those seminal authors would return the book for a full refund. The best academic writing I've seen grapples with groundbreaking theorists, integrates key insights into a distinctive vision, and forges new metaphors and expressions as needed.

SINCERITY VERSUS IRONY

Many authors, academic and otherwise, mistake irony for style. True irony runs deeper than the stylistic surface: it confronts the paradoxes at the core of human existence, gives voice to the pain caused by those inner tensions, and laughs only as a means of facing the pain bravely. To discover ironies just below the surface of experience is to be witty; to discover them *at* the surface is to be glib. Some ironies are so painful that whole societies are in denial about them; the work of exposing those ironies can be the greatest sort of intellectual achievement. But life is so full of ironies that many are free for the taking, and there's nothing more insufferable than a person who belabors an obvious irony as though she were its discoverer. Err on the side of underestimating the originality of the ironies you apprehend, and your wit will automatically temper its tone.

Irony can be a matter of substance, tone, or both. In the award-winning novel *Being Dead*, Jim Crace looks at the lives of his protagonists through the lens of their joint death. A middle-aged pair of doctors of zoology has returned to the sand dunes where they first made love decades earlier, hoping to rekindle their romance. While they're undressing, a mugger strikes each of them in the head with a heavy rock. Here we have linked the two central paradoxes of human life—the evanescence of love that feels eternal and the futility of the life force in us all that strives against death. In fact, love and death are such central ironies that they were formally wed in Romantic German culture as *der Liebestod*, the Love-Death, in which death is seen as the inevitable outcome of great passion. Here, Crace gives us the Love-Death as his two dowdy, soft-bodied scientists might themselves have viewed it:

> The bodies were discovered straightaway. A beetle first. *Claudatus maximi*. A male. Then the raiding parties arrived, drawn by the summons of fresh wounds and the smell of urine: swag flies and crabs, which normally would have to make do with rat dung and the carcasses of fish for their carrion. Then a gull. No one, except the newspapers, could say that "There was only Death amongst the dunes, that summer's afternoon."[1]

By drawing on the victims' own perspective to look at the "after-life" of their corpses, Crace imparts dignity through details that might otherwise seem demeaning. The ironies abound: the *C.*

---

1. Jim Crace, *Being Dead* (New York: Picador, 1999), 36.

maximi beetle is a vegetarian "with no appetite for blood" whose progress is merely interrupted by the falling woman; the bodies, though discovered by dune creatures immediately, aren't found by humans for seven days; the husband's hand has landed on his wife's leg in an accidental consummation of his amorous intentions. None of these reversals of the reader's expectations are played for laughs; the substance is ironic, but the tone is sincere.

In contrast, take David Sedaris's essay "Parade," in which the first-person narrator offhandedly recounts his tumultuous love life while making a guest appearance on Oprah Winfrey's daytime television show. After two pages' worth of funny parody of the high-minded self-involvement that pervades these therapeutic shows, Sedaris ups the stakes: we learn that the show's theme is gay love and that the narrator has had a string of the unlikeliest famous lovers, from Bruce "the Boss" Springsteen to Mike Tyson. Here's a typical passage:

> Charlton Heston and I are finished, and he's hurt. I can understand that, but to tell you the truth, I can't feel sorry for him. He had started getting on my nerves a long time ago, before the *People* story, before our television special, even before that March of Dimes telethon. Charlton can be manipulative and possessive. It seems to have taken me a long time to realize that all along I was in love with the *old* Charlton Heston, the one who stood before the Primate Court of Justice in *Planet of the Apes*. The one who had his loincloth stripped off by Dr. Zaus and who stood there naked and unafraid.[2]

Again, we have multiple layers of irony, multiple reversals of the reader's expectations: Charlton Heston is a well-known con-

---

2. David Sedaris, "Parade," in *Barrel Fever* (Boston: Little, Brown, 1994), 6.

servative and icon of heterosexual masculinity, yet one of his most famous movie moments is indeed a staple of gay camp; contemporary America is hardly likely to embrace a gay couple as the hosts of a telethon; and the narrator's charge of selfishness against his erstwhile lover could clearly be leveled against himself. Here, irony pervades both substance and tone, to hilarious effect. Some might argue that Sedaris's tone is ironic but his content is *satirical*; I'd disagree. Satire does exaggerate a paradox to the point of ridiculousness as here, but it also has a social or political axe to grind, and Sedaris's lighthearted tone clearly means to entertain above all.

Sometimes scholars overlook the most profound ironies in their own discourses. One author documented the startling claim that a famous nineteenth-century archeologist stole credit for discovering a famous city's ruins from a gentleman farmer; later, when she mentioned evidence that the farmer had himself followed another sleuth's clues, the author failed to note the irony of the robbed man's own thievery. A biographer discussed his subject's wish to write a Great American Novel that was not ethnically ghettoized but neglected to remark on the irony that his subject is remembered today chiefly as an ethnic writer. In both cases, the scholars seemed to fear the deeper irony as though it might undermine their thesis; in reality, exploring those depths would only have enriched their discourses.

A complete lack of irony is deadening to most prose. Ironic perception is, to some extent, a gift—it is a sensibility that can be cultivated, but only if the seeds are there. Just as some people are born without a sense of humor, others are missing their irony bone. For those folks, the best bet is to play to their strength, which may be sincerity, honesty, even idealistic fervor. When writing without irony, as when writing *with* irony, the goal is to avoid excess. Err on the side of underestimating the originality of the convictions you hold, and your earnestness will automatically temper its tone.

NARRATIVE VERSUS EXPOSITION

In Chapter 3, I discussed the need to consider the ratio of narrative to exposition in your discourse. There, I focused on the effect these proportions have on the structure of your text; but these two modes also play a determining role in the stylistic choices you make.

To consider the differences, let's return to our roundtable discussion. This time, let's imagine an informal dinner party of which you are the host, the wine flowing liberally, seven courses languorously served. All raconteurs, you and your guests take turns telling entertaining stories. The pediatrician tells about the mother of a patient who thought her thirteen-old-daughter had developed a physical problem with her eyes because recently, whenever her mother spoke to her, the daughter's eyes rolled back into her head. The English professor tells about a female colleague who, tired of being patted on the head by a senior male colleague who liked to roam in and out of departmental meetings, rubbed her feet on the carpet and waited to deliver him a passive-aggressive electrical shock. Laughter flows, and the stories entertain because there are serious themes embedded in them. But the stories don't *lead* anywhere, and eventually the carousel of anecdotes winds down.

On another evening, the same group gathers over an equally sumptuous feast. Because the president is pressing to initiate war on foreign soil to protect U.S. economic interests, the mood is sober. An airline steward working on his M.A. in public health says something about how the pending war will affect his job, and his fatalistic attitude sparks a furor of polite but impassioned discussion. A vigorous debate continues on and off over the course of the evening. When the guests leave, they feel vaguely dissatisfied that the affair was not as pleasurable as the previous dinner party. Yet the effects of the evening linger for days with each participant, and years later it is this party on the eve of war that is best remembered.

In both of these scenarios, the partygoers went home feeling exhausted because of the relentlessness of the mode of conversation. As host, you might have said on the first evening, "So tell me, Clara, do you find gender equity is still a problem on your campus?" On the second evening, you might have filled one of the silences with a story about the day you enlisted, or registered as a conscientious objector. As you revise your dissertation, you'll want to perform similar shifts between narrative and exposition, to keep the discourse focused on its thematic goal but with enough entertaining asides to periodically refresh the reader.

A GLOSSARY OF STYLISTIC ELEMENTS

The following elements are arranged alphabetically to underscore the fact that their importance is not hierarchical. These are the pigments on your color palette, and you'll make your choices at a visceral level, discovering your style as you go. Don't expect to find basic rules of grammar and usage here: the "Syntax" entry is quite brief, and diction is handled under headings of particular relevance to academic prose, such as "Jargon" and "Rhetorical Questions."

For basic guidance in grammar and usage, you must select from among resources that range between two philosophical camps: the descriptivists, who observe patterns of usage as they arise naturally among native speakers; and the prescriptivists, who seek to impose logical rules on speech. According to my descriptivist mentor, Marilyn Schwartz, the *Merriam-Webster's Dictionary of English Usage* is probably the single best authority for unbiased usage information, but she notes that some readers will find this book frustratingly lax. If you're looking to mind all your *p*'s and *q*'s and ensure that the most conservative critic will find no fault with your prose, turn to the recently revised edition of *Fowler's Dictionary of English Usage* or the just-published *Garner's Modern American Usage*, both prescriptivist wolves in descriptivist sheep's clothing. Other resources are listed at the end of this volume.

APHORISM. A generality that is memorable by virtue of its succinctness and wit. The old aphorisms have become clichés, and creating new ones is surprisingly hard work, so aphorisms should be used sparingly. In a recent manuscript, an author who is an authority on evolution said, "In biology, nature abhors a category." Nice. But on the same page, she said, "Color in your salt means fragments of dead shrimp." Umm, excuse me? The first statement works because it wrings a variation on an aphorism already recognizable to us all, "Nature abhors a vacuum." The second statement doesn't work because it assumes that shrimp turning up in one's salt shaker is a universal experience with clear metaphorical resonance.

ATTRIBUTION. Documentation of the source of a quotation or other piece of information. In a book aimed at a broad readership, attribution should be provided as unobtrusively as possible but also keeping in mind the convenience of the reader. Don't make her wonder who is using the familiar expression "keeping up with the Joneses" on page 59; but don't send her back to the notes for that small bit of information, either. Instead, add a clause to the main text that clarifies who said what, reserving footnotes for lengthier "asides" that would otherwise disrupt the flow of your discourse.

CLIFF-HANGER. A suspenseful ending. The term comes from the serials of early cinema, in which the hero was inevitably left dangling one-handed from a cliff or window ledge to ensure that moviegoers returned the following week. Usually cliff-hangers are narrative, but they can be expository as well: that is, a theoretical argument can be interrupted at its apex for dramatic effect. The key to using cliff-hangers effectively is judicious timing: in a nonfiction treatment of serial rape in small-town America, the author broke his narrative up into 76 chapters averaging only three pages in length, then ended each with a cliff-hanger. I found the effect numbing and felt it cheapened the book's sensitive topic by treating it like a daytime soap opera. The author disagreed, and I must admit the book went on to become a bestseller for the publisher—but I maintain his success was in spite of, rather than because of, his gimmick.

COINAGE. Creation of a new technical term. Coining a term is easy; getting it to stick is another matter. Sometimes a new term is sorely needed: I've been working lately with the coiner of the word *geoedaphics*, which refers to plant species that thrive in soils derived from particular geological compounds and processes. The term is precise and allows its user to refer to a complex concept in a few syllables, so it can be forgiven for not falling trippingly off the tongue.

Recently, I reviewed a manuscript in which the author said he would unveil a phenomenon called the "television effect"; what followed was a disparate series of types of effects that television has had on human perception, social institutions, and artistic expression. His coinage—the lynchpin in his claim to intellectual originality—should at the very least have been pluralized, and I confessed to reading his whole manuscript without ever getting a sense of what the "television effect" was.

Before coining a term, ask yourself two questions. First, is the term really filling a need? And second, can you define the term precisely, in one succinct sentence? If you answer yes to both questions, then throw it out there and see if it sticks. See also *De(con)struction*.

COLLOQUIALISM. A word or phrase that smacks of informality and is usually used only in casual conversation. Colloquial phrases can help enliven a text whose subject is inherently dry and technical; they can also undermine the authority of the author's voice. Durable colloquialisms become clichés; but most are ephemeral and will sound dated in a few years. When an author blending jazz criticism with personal memoir wrote of undergoing "heavy-duty stress," or being "scared to death," or "missing a beat," he was adopting a colloquial tone that invited the reader to identify with him as "one of the guys" yet steered clear of both cliché and ephemera. My evolutionary expert used similar phrases quite effectively, but sometimes her striving led her toward cliché: it is well-nigh impossible to put the phrase "whistle a happy tune" to good use in a science text. In a narrative of the lives of people living with AIDS, one author disrupted her otherwise poignant narratives with old saws like "Take two of these and call me in the morning," and "It can be a jungle out there." Acronyms like SOL (for "shit out of luck") are likewise to be avoided. See also *Dialect*.

COMMENTARY. Explication or interpretation of source material. Once the province of literary criticism, this method is prevalent today among oral historians of various disciplinary stripes. When effective, these commentaries resemble the ruminative voice-overs of the narrator in the film *The French Lieutenant's Woman;* when ineffective, they are as relentless as Howard Cosell's play-by-play commentary years ago on Monday Night Football.

The effective commentator provides information that is missing from the source text while avoiding repetition of her subject's own statements. Sometimes the commentator may elaborate an interviewee's comment, clarifying an obscure point or teasing out an implicit meaning, but care must be taken to avoid redundancy. Take, for example, this opening sentence from a paragraph in the oral history of a New Age sect:

> One congregant, a fifty-seven-year-old university professor,
> describes a journey in which doubt does not quite overtake
> his sense of love for the divine.

The reader might expect the quotation to follow here. Instead, the elaboration continues:

> Meaning—some hope of plausibility—rather than intimacy
> has been recovered. The rejection of a spirituality reliant on

prohibitions and judgment has cleared the air but it has not replaced them with a full-blown worldview.

Ready for the quotation now? Not yet:

> In the absence of a fully formed cosmology, this believer is grateful for the significant yet modest vision provided by the general congregation, the central gathering. Hope and meaning, not transcendence over uncertainty, are the cornerstones. There are no global harmonies, no epiphanies.

Ah, finally the quotation itself, which does indeed make all of these points. But why bother reading it? The extract has been robbed of its purpose, not to mention its piquancy. See also *Editorialization*.

DE(CON)STRUCTION. The process of identifying the assumptions implicit in language and other cultural constructs. Deconstruction is one of the most powerful tools developed by the postmodernists. It has laid bare the misogyny and homophobia at the core of patriarchal society, eliminated the boundary between art and reality, and reconnected us with our linguistic roots. The deconstructivist would rather die than impose meaning; instead, she wants to "complicate our understanding" of cultural constructs we think we already understand by breaking them down into their fundamental elements.

Unfortunately, most deconstructivists are better thinkers than writers, and the theory industry of the 1980s and 1990s saw many embarrassing coinages go into print. I can remember refereeing an exchange between an author and copyeditor as to whether there were shades of meaning among *(en)gender, en/gender,* and *en-*

gender. The author intended this word to serve simultaneously as two verbs, *to gender* and *to engender,* while also showing how notions of gender are implicit in all acts of human creation. Once a form was settled on, the author resisted limiting the word's use— she passionately believed that repetition of phrases in their deconstructed form was necessary to counteract millennia of patriarchal brainwashing. The copy editor was sympathetic but pointed out that many of the sentences in which *en/gender* appeared could not be read meaningfully with both verbs: in most cases, either *engender* or *gender* was truly meant.

The bottom line: at the sentence level, employ deconstruction—or de(con)struction—very selectively, as you would other coinages. See also *Coinage.*

DIALECT. A regional, ethnic, socioeconomic, or generational variant of a language. The differences between a dialect and its parent language include both pronunciation and diction. Colloquialisms usually begin as phrases in a dialect, then spread either because of their aptness or because a new generation wishes to make itself heard afresh. When dialect appears in scholarly writing, it usually does so sparingly to enliven the text and reflect the regional or ethnic flavor of the subject. My jazz memoirist used the phrase "shine me on" to refer to cussing a person out: it's still unclear to me whether the phrase was specific to his native Milwaukee or current throughout African American culture, but he made its meaning clear from context and marked it off with quotation marks.

Aside from such occasional phrases, dialect in scholarly writing appears mainly in the block quotations recorded by oral historians. Here, care should be exercised when conveying differences in pronunciation. "Wha' chu wanna do?" may be exactly how the black jazz musician spoke, but transcribing his pronunciation with rigid fidelity and then allowing other characters, who are white or more highly educated, to say "What do you want to do?" would be racist, classist, or both. No native speaker of English pronounces every syllable of that sentence unless with strained deliberation during an argument. See also *Colloquialism*.

DIALOGUE. Direct speech between two or more conversants. In academic writing, dialogue is likely to appear only in dramatizations or when an oral historian recounts discussions with or among her subjects. Dialogue should be set off clearly in quotation marks. Don't be afraid to use simple attributions like "he said" and "she said" repeatedly. A reader following a dialogue doesn't see these phrases as repetitive but merely takes them as cues, like speakers' initials in a script. Words like *chortled*, *threatened*, *chided*, and *whispered* should be employed only when they are truly apt; a dialogue littered with them comes across as cheap melodrama. And adverbs—"he chortled archly"—are to be avoided at all costs.

DRAMATIZATION. Evoking a narrative scene in the midst of expository discourse. Done well, this technique can enliven your discussion; done poorly, it can cause confusion or give rise to unwanted chuckles. In her prepublication review of a manuscript that built a case for an obscure historical figure as the "precursor to Jesus," one scholar complained that her colleague's reconstruction of a day in the life of his subject was "too vivid." I disagreed—as a nonspecialist, I found the author's few dramatic set pieces the most engaging pages in the text, which was largely devoted to arcane exegesis of passages from the Dead Sea Scrolls. The problem seemed to be that these dramatizations were sprung on the reader unawares; the connection to the exposition was unclear. I recommended that the dramatic scenes be coordinated with the organizational structure of the manuscript, with one such scene either opening or closing each chapter.

EDITORIALIZATION. Making interpretive remarks. Whereas commentary provides interpretation in complete thoughts, editorializing conveys an author's point of view more subtly, via words and phrases colored with judgment. If your text is purposely polemical, then editorializing is your modus operandi and can be put to extremely effective use. If your goal is to treat your subject from a balanced perspective, then editorializing will undermine your reader's confidence in your project.

Often, writers editorialize inadvertently when searching for a colorful adjective: authors writing about interfaith ecumenism spoke of a Catholic religious order's "dour asceticism," suggesting a negative attitude toward a key component of the devout life that they may or may not have intended. They also betrayed a prejudice against monks who incorporated non-Christian elements into their belief systems with phrases like "random concoctions," "religious tourism," "New Age ruminations," "magpie habits," and "emotional bravura" with "a low-life tinge."

When you reach for a colorful word or phrase, make it a concrete one. My authors could have conveyed much more about the effects of interfaith ecumenism on their monks by describing the cell of one subject, in which perhaps a miniature Zen garden sat on the desk and a crystal hung in the window. These details would have allowed the reader to make up her own mind about the monk's lifestyle: some readers would have thought to themselves, "How blasphemous and ridiculous," while others would have thought, "How cool!" See also *Commentary*.

EPIGRAPHS. Brief quotations used in display headings to suggest a theme or themes. Epigraphs may appear at the beginning of a book, as well as at the head of each chapter and even, in some cases, each subsection. Epigraphs, like chapter titles and other display matter, are intended to entice the reader into the text, and their effective deployment is a minor art form. Most academic authors use epigraphs too liberally and for the wrong reason, namely, as a means of elevating the status of Particularly Important Block Quotations. They'll stack three to five extracts at the head of each chapter, insert more at each subhead, and allow them to run on for several sentences apiece. In a work synthesizing oral history, this liberal use can be appropriate, but in most books greater restraint is called for.

Now imagine that you are writing a book on the effects of political revolution on European art in the twentieth century. Your first impulse might be to select the most capacious umbrella for your theme; at the head of your introduction, for instance, you might place this single epigraph:

> If an important impulse behind experimentation in the arts
> at the turn of the century was a quest for liberation, a break,
> in aesthetic and moral terms, from central authority[,] . . .
> from bourgeois conformity[,] . . . then it was no surprise that
> much of the psychological and spiritual momentum for this
> break came from the peripheries, geographical, social, gen-
> erational, and sexual. (Modris Eksteins, *Rites of Spring*,
> 1989)

Your choice gives only muted voice to the exhilarating drama that attended this "important impulse." Now consider the effect if you were to use instead these two epigraphs:

> I have passed like a madman through the slippery-floored halls of museums. . . . The enchantments that the street outside had to offer me were a thousand times more real.
> (André Breton, "Surrealism and Painting," 1928)

> There is nothing more dangerous than justice in the hands of judges, and a paintbrush in the hands of a painter.
> (Picasso, *Conversation*, 1935)

An epigraph is an opportunity for the bookstore browser to "eavesdrop" on the narrative, to register dramatic tensions that will draw her in. See also *Headings*.

FOREIGN TERMS. Words and phrases originating in languages other than English that have not entered common American usage. A quick way to determine whether a foreign phrase has been assimilated into American English is to check whether it occurs as a main entry in *Webster's Collegiate Dictionary*, 11th edition, or whether it appears in the back under "Foreign Words and Phrases." The former need not be italicized (per diem, weltanschauung, kamikaze, ad hoc); the latter should be *(bon appétit, Lebenswelt, par exemple, post hoc)*.

In general, the broader the readership you desire, the less you should pepper your text with untranslated foreign terms. Translations for all but the most obvious terms should be appended parenthetically at first occurrence. When weeding out unnecessary foreign terms, look for those that can be said as succinctly in English and with minimal loss of connotation. In those instances, place the foreign term in parentheses at the first occurrence of the English equivalent.

HAGIOGRAPHY. Uncritically positive treatment of a human subject. The term is adopted from religious studies and literally means "the biography of a saint." In academic writing, hagiography is often subtle, showing through as a degree of admiration for the author's subject that weakens the reader's confidence in her critical judgment. An author of the biography of a medical pioneer called his subject, over the course of twenty manuscript pages, a "genius" who "dares to be great" and "one of those modern truth seekers" who nevertheless was "gracious and caring," with a "knack for organization and leadership" and "a fine sense of humor." Doubtless all of these statements were valid, but their tone was so friendly that they fostered misgivings. The scientist's famous brashness, aggressiveness, and disregard for protocols seemed to be apologized for, and the reader didn't hear the voices of many critics, although it seems the scientist had many. In an authorized biography, the author may have little discretion in the use of critical sources, but the warmest and fuzziest phrases should be excised so that the appearance of partiality is at least minimized.

HEADINGS. Part titles, chapter titles, and subheads. Like epigraphs, these other "display elements" are important tools in attracting and keeping a reader's attention, but headings have the added mission of conveying the content's structure clearly and accurately. Most academic authors err on the side of accuracy with titles that are intimidatingly long and broad: "Community, Hierarchy, and Authority: Elites and Nonelites in the Making of

Native-Place Culture during the Late Qing." There's nothing wrong with this chapter title, but it doesn't *sing*. Consider a title of equal length from another Asian studies title: "The Forbidden Chrysanthemum: Male-Male Sexuality in Meiji Legal Discourse." Both titles have a lot of information to impart, but the latter is more appealing because it takes a few extra words to establish a tone, an atmosphere.

When revising their dissertations, many authors take the advice of their editors to heart and prune their headings but in the process pare them down too far. My evolutionary expert had subheadings like "Bizarre?" and "Implications"; these gave the reader no clue as to what content would follow. Some academics are prone to employing quotations as titles; unless very apt, most quotations will not provide enough specificity to be useful as titles. Consider one less-than-scintillating chapter title in an author's manuscript on civil rights: "All Over the Entire State of Florida." What could be more bland? If using quotations in headings is your preferred strategy, find pithy ones; this author overlooked such compelling choices as "Stand Like Men or Die Like Dogs" and "The Peculiar Disposition of Blacks." See also *Epigraphs*; *Quotation*.

HUMOR. Content or tone that provides amusement. Authors of books on serious subjects should err on the side of caution when incorporating humorous remarks into their text. The author of the manuscript on the "television effect" had a likable voice overall, but his humor was slightly heavy-handed. He opened with a joke that was stale and too long in the telling; later, he demonstrated questionable taste by speculating that Muhammad Ali might have "taken too many blows to the head" to be able to appreciate the irony of a soft drink commercial in which his younger self sparred in the ring with his daughter Laila, herself a professional boxer. There was just a little too much elbow nudging, as when the author said, "The duel, by the way, never materialized"—at this point, the reader knew that neither opponent in the conflict had had the nerve to actually fight, and the irony here would have been subtler if the phrase "by the way" had been deleted. Puns are to be avoided.

JARGON. Terms used within a specialized field of study. In their first books, most scholars part with their jargon reluctantly because they are anxious to demonstrate that they've mastered the canonical literature. Writing later in their careers, senior scholars sometimes relax their diction in order to broaden their readership, but as often they don't, fretting instead that they will "dumb down" their argument should they simplify their language. This defense of jargon often masks an author's insecurity about her writing ability—at a subconscious level, she knows that it takes much greater skill to write in a manner that both stimulates specialists and enlightens nonspecialists than it does to rehearse ready-made phrases.

True, jargon can have its charm. This past year, I've developed a style sheet for a series of natural history guides to the flora and fauna of California; in it, I erred by prescribing that the biologist's quaint use of *character* be changed to *characteristic* during copyediting. A hue and cry arose among the series authors; from mycologists to mammalogists, they considered *character* one of those "in" usages that help to give their community a sense of identity. Many grew up in California and can remember how, as young boys and girls, they savored the unfamiliar words in field guides, feeling themselves admitted into magical arcane worlds.

When revising your dissertation, aspire to dumb your argument *up*. Reduce the amount of jargon by retaining only those specialist terms that cannot be summed up in equally concise lay language or that convey nuances that would be lost in translation. Don't mistake the formality of Latinate roots for nuance: *ovate* means "egg-shaped" and not much else. Where a technical term is apt, work clues to its definition into the sentence in which it appears so that readers from outside your field can gather its meaning from context.

Assumption of specialist knowledge can extend beyond terms of art. Another civil rights historian expected her lay readers to remember events, political parties, and landmark court cases from their junior high history lessons. My memory lobe tingled at the sight of references to the Chicago Race Riot, Bourbon Democrats, and *Plessy v. Ferguson*, but I couldn't recall enough of their import to follow her discourse. She also was fond of namedropping, which is fine for the Alexis de Tocquevilles of the world but not for the Kenneth Wiggins Porters. In this regard, *Webster's Collegiate* can be a useful guide: if a person is famous enough to appear in that dictionary's terse biographical section, then she or he probably does not need to be glossed for the reader. Otherwise, a phrase of introduction is only polite.

METAPHOR. The expression of an abstract concept in concrete terms. In poetics, metaphor can express one concrete phenomenon in terms of another—lovemaking as eating at a feast—but in academic writing the main use of metaphor is to clothe ethereal thoughts in memorable images. In all metaphor, one set of human experiences is mapped onto another: eating onto lovemaking, nightfall onto sadness, nervous excitement onto a hummingbird's flight. When the distance between the two mapped sets of experience is great, the metaphor is original; when the number of shared qualities between the two mapped sets is great, the metaphor is apt. The greatest metaphors are those that are both original and apt—but this combination is a tough feat to pull off, because most of the great metaphors have already been taken.

Consider feasting as a metaphor for lovemaking—it is so good it became a cliché back in the Dark Ages. On the other end of the spectrum, consider these lines from a poem by Yehuda Amichai (as translated by Chana Bloch and Stephen Mitchell): "We were such a good and loving invention: an airplane made of a man and woman, wings and all." Here, the juxtaposition of aircraft and conjugal union works because we discover, to our great surprise, that these two seemingly disparate sets of human experience actually have much in common: the elation of flight; the sense of large parts having been welded into a whole; even shape—we see one partner on top of the other, legs straight, arms stretched wide and hands clasped in passion. Of course, the originality of the metaphor owes much to the modernity of the airplane image—Homer didn't have access to both sets of experience referenced by Amichai, else this metaphor might have turned cliché millennia ago.

When academic authors have trouble with metaphor, it's usually because they've pushed in the direction of originality and gone too far. One author combined mice and bowling pins with unsavory results; another wrote of the "long, partisan arm" of a government agency; and another placed the sky underfoot ("the firmament is shifting out from under them"). In these cases, the sets of experience mapped onto each other are mutually exclusive: a human bicep, elbow, and forearm can't be "partisan." Such a metaphor is said to be *mixed*.

Sometimes the metaphors themselves are fine but their deployment is mishandled. In a long passage in which she lucidly explained the complex interactions of sexually significant chemicals, my evolutionist suddenly switched her central metaphor from an orchestra to a committee; both were apt, but she needed to choose one or the other and stick with it.

Purists will note that I've made no distinction between metaphor and simile. Technically, a simile is an explicit comparison ("she was pretty as a picture"), metaphor an implicit one ("she was a pretty picture"). In grade school, we were taught that a simile is a metaphor that uses "like" or "as," but this reductive distinction is of little use. Consider this line from Amichai: "The air over Jerusalem is saturated with prayers and dreams / like the air over industrial cities." Metaphor or simile? Doesn't matter. The freshness of the layered comparisons is what strikes the reader. Similes are best used when the comparison is so unusual that making it explicit is desirable for clarity, or when multiple comparisons appear in a sentence or paragraph. Again, watch Amichai, the master: "Love is finished again, like a profitable citrus season, / or like an archeological dig that turned up / from deep inside the earth / turbulent things that wanted to be forgotten."

NARRATIVE DETAIL. Concrete language evoking people, places, and events. This technique is closely allied with dramatization. In his memoir, a paleontologist begins one chapter by describing a visit to a cave located partway down the wall of a deep canyon. He and his companions are conveyed to the cave in a steel bucket that steeply descends a long cable, and the author can't help describing his nervousness, or the smell of the guano once they arrive. Yet while dangling over the canyon, rather than evoke the wind in his face or the creaking of the cable, he fantasizes about the fossils he hopes to find at the cable's end! This example says much about the single-mindedness of the scientific mind, but it also demonstrates the tendency of specialist authors to get so caught up in the scholarly import of their subject matter that they forget to draw the reader into their excitement.

When an author first mentions a person, place, or thing that will figure significantly in her narrative, she should take a sentence or two to fix it in the reader's memory with physical details. Facial features, manner of speaking, manner of comportment and dress—these elements not only stimulate the reader's interest but also help her to keep track of a large cast of characters.

Some authors provide vivid descriptions of others but leave themselves in the shadows when they figure into their own narratives as characters. This flaw surfaces most noticeably in "professional memoirs," but authors writing earlier in their careers often make the same mistake when they place themselves in their narratives for the purpose of acknowledging the influence of their video recorders, say, on the atmosphere of a ritual in a Papua New Guinean village. These anthropologists pride themselves on awareness of their subjective selves, yet they stint on description of their own bodies, voices, and clothing. Others carry self-exposure to the other extreme, writing an entire discourse on patriarchy and female gender that turns out to be the story of the author's doomed love affair with an unethical professor. Strike a balance, but don't neglect physical description of any of your main characters, including yourself.

QUOTATION. Use of the words of another. The intermingling of other voices with one's own in prose is no less an art than harmonizing in musical performance. Too few quotations, and the audience grows bored with the endless aria of your voice; too many, and your solo is drowned out by the chorus. First-time academic authors often quote excessively to demonstrate their recent mastery of their field's literature: this hyperattribution is acceptable in a dissertation but should be removed from the text before publication in book form. Before using a quotation, ask yourself: Does this person say it better than I could? Does this person's authority lend weight to a point that might otherwise be disputed? Does this passage have room for another quotation? If the answer to any of these questions is "No," paraphrase.

Some authors err in the opposite direction. Reading the biography of a famous playwright, I was astonished to find that the manuscript contained almost no direct quotation from the playwright's work. The author provided plot synopses of his subject's major novels, stories, and plays and sometimes drew parallels between the fictional characters and the people in the playwright's life, but he didn't allow the reader direct access to the playwright's voice, much less the voices of the characters in the literary works. If you find yourself paraphrasing whole conversations, revisit your quotation strategy.

RHETORICAL ENUMERATION. Explicit numbering of theses, themes, or concepts. Often an effective means of navigating diverse concepts, when used too frequently this device degrades the organizational clarity of a manuscript. One book introduction contained two "musts," two attitudes, two hypotheses, two reasons, three important respects—and a partridge in a pear tree. The reader felt as though she should be keeping track of all these dualities, but the author didn't revisit the concepts, so the reader's effort did not pay off. On one page, for instance, the introduction of three kinds of medical entrepreneurs made me think these distinctions would be important to later discussion, but they weren't. In humanities texts, and science texts aimed at a broad audience, enumeration should be used as sparingly as possible, and only when the enumerated topics clearly benefit by their classification as part of a group. See also *Rhetorical Questions*.

RHETORICAL QUESTIONS. Questions to which no answer is expected. This device smacks of the pulpit and should be used very sparingly; just a few rhetorical questions can cast a pall of hectoring over an entire chapter. One author who was particularly fond of these would pose questions in long strings, then provide answers in an order other than that of the questions. The reader ended up with the nagging feeling that she'd missed some important connections. Some writers use rhetorical questions for the wrong reasons: they want to bring up a topic but don't want to address it fully. At other times the question is a benign conjecture that adds little weight to the discourse: What would Lindbergh have thought of the space shuttle? The bottom line: avoid rhetorical questions unless you're writing a valedictory address. See also *Rhetorical Enumeration*.

SARCASM. A bitter or hurtful remark; sometimes confused with irony. An ironic remark can be delivered sarcastically, but a sarcastic tone does not guarantee ironic insight. Stylistically speaking, an irony is a figure of speech that says the opposite of what it
 to cleverly unveil a contradiction; sarcasm may employ

irony, but its main purpose is to inflict a stinging blow. When Jack, the outlandish best friend in the television situation comedy *Will and Grace*, responds to a clever jibe of Will's by saying, "Oh yeah? Well, you're fat," we laugh because we recognize that this bitchiness doesn't match his friend's wit (not to mention the fact that Will is as skinny as a rail). In my experience, true sarcasm is relatively rare in scholarship; it most often surfaces accidentally, when an author strives to be witty and instead inadvertently offends. See also *Editorialization* and "Sincerity versus Irony," above.

SYNTAX. The arrangement of words into phrases and sentences. Academic authors have a reputation for writing long, convoluted sentences, but in my experience the opposite tendency prevails: many authors today aspiring to the simplicity and clarity of journalism adopt a tone that is staccato in its lockstep conformity to a handful of sentence patterns. When prose contains few compound sentences and only brief modifying clauses, one of two explanations is likely: either the author is a master of lucidity, or her prose doesn't reflect much critical thinking. Critical thinking usually gives rise to oblique connections, incursions, and reversals that become embodied in lithe sentence patterns. The key ingredient to masterful syntax is variation: from shorter paragraph to longer, from simpler sentence to more complex, from paraphrase to direct quotation. In this dappled light, an author's native journalistic succinctness will stand out as the virtue it is.

I'll close with another table story. It's 7:30 A.M., and I'm sitting in a dining room overlooking the Berkeley marina across from a man in his mid-seventies. Blue-eyed and white-haired, he's just completed a half-mile swim in the hotel's lap pool and now plows into his eggs, bacon, and hash browns with impunity. He's invited me to breakfast to thank me for my copyediting: "I know good editing when I see it," he wrote weeks earlier in an e-mail message. The response came as a great relief because I'd made some strong suggestions to moderate a tone that was unduly argumentative.

While we eat, a woman in Sunday clothes approaches our table for an autograph. She has a copy of my companion's latest romance novel in hand and beams like a teenage rock-and-roll groupie while he signs it. He's the most famous author I'm likely ever to work with, a cultural anthropologist by training who has made his field observations do double duty, producing from each excursion among the *indígenas* both a specialist treatise and a bodice-ripping adventure story. The novels have sold fifteen million copies and counting, the treatises barely a thousandth of that number.

"Always time for a pretty lady," he drawls. It's a sexist remark, delivered just a mile from the epicenter of political correctness, yet the woman and I are both disarmed by the twinkle in his eye, which flashes the message, "I know I'm misbehaving."

"They're all jealous, you realize," he muses aloud, after she's gone. "My academic colleagues. They don't see how my novels and nonfiction come out of the same impulse. The novels are explorations of the soul, and the treatises deal with facts, but they are both versions of the same truths."

Maybe, but in your novels you woo your readers, whereas in your treatises you kvetch and bicker. I think this but say nothing—the forthrightness with which I queried his manuscript fails me now.

When the table has been cleared, he presents me with a signed clothbound copy of his latest novel. "It's my best cover yet," he says, and I can only nod in mute wonder at the raised-foil lettering, his name larger than the two-word title. In the years since, seeing his novels at airports and checkout counters, I've come to a useful realization: that each new piece of writing is a fresh conversation between author and audience, and each requires a fresh effort at establishing rapport. In his popular novels, my breakfast companion makes that effort with every new outing and reliably delivers an irascible charm; but in each treatise, he responds testily to the mixed reviews of his previous monograph, so that his tone grows more embattled over time.

As you begin revising your dissertation, you are faced with a similar challenge. You don't have to turn your serious discourse into a swashbuckling yarn, but you do need to have a fresh conversation with your readers. Whatever style comes naturally to you—sincerity or irony, humor or sobriety, drama or understatement—you need to get some of your own self onto the page.

5

TIME TO TRIM

NOTES, BIBLIOGRAPHIES, TABLES, AND GRAPHS

Jenya Weinreb

> The aesthetic evil of a footnote seems in order
> just here, I'm afraid.
>
> J. D. Salinger,
> *Franny and Zooey*

Book editors groan when they see the phrase "revised dissertation" in a proposal. The words bring to mind a manuscript heavy
with scholarly apparatus. In this chapter I discuss how to revise
and trim your notes, bibliographies, tables, and graphs to shape a
book that is authoritative but not pedantic.

I thank designer Mary Valencia for her help with the figures in this chapter.
I am grateful to Laura Jones Dooley and Mary Pasti for their wise editorial advice.

WHY CUT?

Having just spent months or years completing a dissertation, you may be understandably reluctant to delete a large chunk of it. There are several reasons why publishers ask scholars to trim notes and omit tables.

First and most important is the question of audience. Thesis writers are encouraged to display all that they have learned in the course of painstaking research. They must prove to their committee that no source has gone unconsulted. All relevant documents—interviews, archival materials, primary sources—should be presented, all previous theories considered.

In a book, documentation has a different purpose: to assist the reader. The author is a full-fledged scholar, the expert on the topic at hand. He or she does not need to demonstrate mastery of the subject. On the contrary, readers count on the author to distill all the available information and present what is most important. As a result, much of the supporting material in a thesis would be considered excessive, even counterproductive, in a book.

The audience for a book is (at least in theory) wider than the audience for a thesis. The audience for a thesis is, most narrowly, the thesis committee and, more broadly, other researchers in the field. But most books, even scholarly ones, seek to inform, convince, or intrigue readers outside that restricted group. A thesis on landscape in Jane Austen's work might be intended only for scholars of nineteenth-century literature, but a book on that topic could appeal to the entire English department and to researchers in art history, landscape architecture, and archeology as well. That wider audience would be daunted to find ten citations where one would do—and those in your field who read the book may well be familiar with all ten and would like to know which one you consider most relevant.

So one reason to trim is to convert the documentation from a proof of expertise into an aid to the reader. A second, related reason to cut scholarly apparatus is to enhance the narrative flow. To attract that wider audience, you need to draw readers in and keep them interested. Abundant note numbers, parenthetical author-date citations, tables, and graphs all interrupt the argument; they are distracting.

This brings us to a third reason to limit academic apparatus, and it is a purely pragmatic, economic one. Fewer notes and references mean fewer pages, which result in lower editing, typesetting, and printing costs and thus a lower cover price—and again, a wider audience. Tables and graphs can be particularly expensive to typeset, so it makes financial sense to keep them to a minimum. A book that is economical to produce will be easier to pitch to a publisher than one that represents a larger financial risk.

Finally, including extensive documentation increases the chances that an error—say, in citing a peripheral source—could creep into the final product. An inadvertent mistake could, if caught, damage your credibility or, if not caught, be reproduced by other scholars.

SYSTEMS OF DOCUMENTATION

In revising a dissertation, then, you should eliminate unnecessary citations. Rather than ask what to get rid of, it makes sense first to ask what must be kept.

- The source of a direct quotation must be given.
- The origin of an opinion or conclusion, if not the author's own, should be acknowledged.
- Credit must be provided for any large or complete pieces of material—extensive quotations, tables, or figures—taken from previously published work, and permission must be obtained to reprint.

Anything that doesn't fit into one of those categories is optional. Be firm in deciding what citations to eliminate:

- Statements of fact need not be referenced unless they are under dispute, presented as discoveries, or seen in a new context.
- Discursive notes that bear little relation to the text should be deleted.
- Discursive notes that are crucial to the argument should be incorporated into the text.

Most publishers consider several systems of documentation to be acceptable in book manuscripts. The three most workable are the endnote system (sometimes called the humanities system), the author-date system, and the unnumbered-note system.

ENDNOTES AND BIBLIOGRAPHIES

The endnote system is commonly used in the humanities.[1] Unlike the author-date system (discussed below), it can accommodate any kind of citation with equal ease, and when used properly, it is

1. The endnote system and the author-date system are explained in great detail in *The Chicago Manual of Style*, 15th ed. (Chicago: University of Chicago Press,

more elegant, because the text is uninterrupted by parenthetical citations.

The endnotes, numbered beginning with 1 in each chapter, appear at the back of the book, keyed to raised note numbers (superscripts) within the text itself. These end-of-book notes are not the same as end-of-*chapter* notes, which are generally reserved for multiauthor collections of essays. As for foot-of-page notes, or footnotes, most book publishers avoid them because they cause complications in page makeup and, even in the digital age, are generally more costly to typeset than endnotes. Footnotes may be preferred, however, in a few cases—for example, to define difficult terms in a foreign-language textbook or to gloss unfamiliar words in a scholarly edition of Shakespeare. They are rarely appropriate in a revised thesis.

Endnotes make for a less cluttered page, but even when the notes appear at the back there is reason to limit their number. A page of text peppered with superscripts looks pedantic and cluttered. How frustrating, too, for the reader who flips to the notes at the back of the book only to find a string of *ibid.*'s. Notes can be combined, shortened, or eliminated in several ways:

- Include several citations in one note. If there are three quotations in a paragraph, the reader will deduce that the first citation goes to the first quotation, the second to the second, and the third to the third.
- For frequently cited works, insert a note upon first mention and use parenthetical page numbers in the text there-

---

2003). The following discussion of those systems relies heavily on this essential resource.

after. In addition, use abbreviations in the notes to prevent repetition of lengthy citations.

1. Judith Rich Harris, *The Nurture Assumption* (New York: Free
Press, 1998), 33. In the following discussion, page numbers
given in the text refer to this work.

2. Child Welfare League of America, Social Welfare History
Archives, University of Minnesota, Minneapolis (hereafter
cited as CWLA), box 21, folder 9.

3. Stephen Pinker, *The Language Instinct* (New York: Harper-
Collins, 1994); CWLA, box 21, folder 9.[2]

- Keep discursive (that is, amplifying or explanatory) notes
to a bare minimum. If a note is peripheral to your argument, get rid of it. If it is too important to delete, make it
part of the text.

- Some citations—of newspaper articles, legal cases, interviews, and so on—can be worked into the text, obviating
the need for a note.

- Quotations almost never need to appear both in their
original language and in English translation. Get rid of
the original (assuming you are writing for an English-
speaking audience) and give the source of the translation.
One note stating "unless otherwise indicated, all translations are my own"—placed after the first quotation—may
be all that's called for.

When revising, aim for no more than one note per paragraph,
and certainly include no more than one note per sentence. The

---

2. Unless otherwise noted, the examples given in this chapter are my invention.

following example shows how a paragraph with five notes (in the first version) can be reduced to two (in the second).

> Most network users agree that writing styles are somehow transformed by the computer. In a survey by Ruth Ryan, 95 percent of respondents "indicated they had encountered differences in communication using computer-mediated communication as opposed to face-to-face or traditional print methods."[1] According to Bay Area Women in Telecommunications, however, in 1993 only 10 to 15 percent of the users on many computer systems were women.[2] Why? Possibly because much technology is designed by and for men.[3] Although Sherry Turkle and Seymour Papert believe that "discrimination in the computer culture . . . is determined not by rules that keep people out but by ways of thinking that make them reluctant to join in,"[4] Paul Edwards maintains that computers are built to resist women's efforts to "make friends" with them.[5]

> 1. Ruth Ryan, "International Connectivity: A Survey of Attitudes about Cultural and National Differences Encountered in Computer-Mediated Communication," *Online Chronicle of Distance Education and Communication* 6, no. 1 (1992), http://www.eff.org/Net_culture/Infotopia/culture_and_comp_mediation.paper.

> 2. Hoai-An Truong, "Gender Issues in Online Communications," 1993, version 4.3, with additional writing and editing by Gail Williams, Judi Clark, and Anna Couey, in conjunction with members of Bay Area Women in Telecommunications, http://www.cpsr.org/cpsr/gender/bawit.cfp93.

> 3. Judy Smith and Ellen Balka, "Chatting on a Feminist Computer Network," in *Technology and Women's Voices: Keeping in Touch*, ed. Cheris Kramarae (New York: Routledge and Kegan Paul, 1988), 82.

> 4. Sherry Turkle and Seymour Papert, "Epistemological Pluralism: Styles and Voices within the Computer Culture,"

Signs: Journal of Women in Culture and Society 16, no. 1
(1990): 132.

5. Paul N. Edwards, "From 'Impact' to Social Process: Com-
puters in Society and Culture," in *Handbook of Science and
Technology Studies*, ed. Sheila Jasanoff, Gerald E. Markle,
James C. Peterson, and Trevor Pinch (Thousand Oaks,
Calif.: Sage Publications, 1995).

The first two notes can be combined, the third deleted, and the
last two combined:

Most network users agree that writing styles are somehow
transformed by the computer. In a survey by Ruth Ryan, 95
percent of respondents "indicated they had encountered
differences in communication using computer-mediated
communication as opposed to face-to-face or traditional
print methods." According to Bay Area Women in Telecommunications, however, in 1993 only 10 to 15 percent of the
users on many computer systems were women.[1] Why? Possibly because much technology is designed by and for men. Although Sherry Turkle and Seymour Papert believe that "dis-
crimination in the computer culture . . . is determined not by
rules that keep people out but by ways of thinking that make
them reluctant to join in," Paul Edwards maintains that computers are built to resist women's efforts to "make friends"
with them.[2]

1. Ruth Ryan, "International Connectivity: A Survey of Attitudes about Cultural and National Differences Encountered in Computer-Mediated Communication," *Online
Chronicle of Distance Education and Communication* 6, no. 1
(1992), http://www.eff.org/Net_culture/Infotopia/
culture_and_comp_mediation.paper; for Bay Area Women
in Telecommunications statistics, see Hoai-An Truong,
"Gender Issues in Online Communications," 1993, version
4.3, with additional writing and editing by Gail Williams,
Judi Clark, and Anna Couey, in conjunction with members

of Bay Area Women in Telecommunications,
http://www.cpsr.org/cpsr/gender/bawit.cfp93.

2. Sherry Turkle and Seymour Papert, "Epistemological Pluralism: Styles and Voices within the Computer Culture,"
Signs: Journal of Women in Culture and Society 16, no. 1
(1990): 132; Paul N. Edwards, "From 'Impact' to Social
Process: Computers in Society and Culture," in *Handbook
of Science and Technology Studies*, ed. Sheila Jasanoff, Gerald
E. Markle, James C. Peterson, and Trevor Pinch (Thousand Oaks, F Sage Publications, 1995).

Do not attach superscripts to chapter titles, epigraphs, headings, or other elements that are set off from the text. Titles and
headings are often set in large or bold type, making superscripts
look awkward. It is standard practice instead to place a superscript
at the end of the first sentence after a heading. Epigraph sources
are generally given with the epigraph; only author and title (and
sometimes a date) are desirable. The epigraph to this chapter provides an example. If an epigraph is taken from an unusual
source—say, a letter—more amplification may be required. In
that case, the source may be given in an unnumbered note pre-
ceding the first note in the chapter.

The preface of a book is itself a note to the text and thus should
not contain additional notes. If a quotation appears in the preface,
its source can be given in parentheses immediately thereafter. If
a preface includes many quotations, it is probably not really a
preface but rather an introduction.

For the format of the notes themselves, you cannot go wrong
by consulting *The Chicago Manual of Style*. Some fields have their
own style guide (for example, many law-related books follow the
Harvard Law Review's *Bluebook* citation format), which may be
used if appropriate for the nature of the book, its audience, and

the house style of the publisher. Regardless of the style, it is imperative to be consistent.

Not all books with notes need bibliographies. It is acceptable—in some cases, preferable—to do without a bibliography if each source is cited in full upon first mention in each chapter. (Some authorities say that it is sufficient to give the complete source only once in the entire book, but that practice requires readers to be more diligent in their search for publication information.) The addition of a bibliography means more pages and thus higher production costs, possibly raising the price of the book. It must be worth the expense. In a book, the purpose of a bibliography is not to prove that the author has consulted all the relevant literature. Rather, the bibliography is a tool for the reader who wishes to conduct further research. If it is to be useful, it should contain only those resources that either the general reader or the specialist will want and be able to consult. If readers will be able to find sources easily in the notes (and they may well be able to, because you've already cut half of them, right?), drop the bibliography and save yourself the time it takes to trim it.

If you decide that a bibliography is warranted, act as the reader's gatekeeper and point the way only to the resources that you found most worthwhile. This may mean eliminating two-thirds of the references cited in your thesis. If you do include a bibliography, you can also trim the notes even further: there is no need to cite a source in full if it is listed in the bibliography. Use a short form (author, shortened title, page number) even the first time the source is cited. Do not duplicate in the notes the information that is found in the bibliography. For example, the two notes given above would become a fraction of their former size:

1. Ryan, "International Connectivity"; for Bay Area Women in Telecommunications statistics, see Truong, "Gender Issues in Online Communications."
2. Turkle and Papert, "Epistemological Pluralism," 132; Edwards, "From 'Impact' to Social Process."

A bibliography typically should not be divided into sections. One alphabetical list is almost always best. If a reader wants to find out what D. H. Lawrence had to say on the subject of the American Southwest, he or she doesn't want to have to wade through thirty pages to find citations to one magazine article, several diary entries, and multiple volumes of letters. There are exceptions, however: in a book about a little-known nineteenth-century feminist, for example, it may make sense to list archives separately from secondary sources. The key is to anticipate how the reader will use the bibliography.

An alternative to the traditional bibliography is a bibliographic essay, in which the author guides the reader toward the most relevant information. It is appropriate only if it provides more information than a straightforward list would, but a well-crafted bibliographic essay allows the author's point of view and personality to shine through:

> John Willinsky explains much in his rather ill-tempered *Empire of Words — The Reign of the OED* (Princeton: Princeton University Press, 1994), which offers a politically correct revisionist view of James Murray's creation—albeit from a somewhat admiring stance. It is worth reading, even if just to make one's blood boil.[3]

3. Simon Winchester, *The Professor and the Madman: A Tale of Murder, Insanity, and the Making of the "Oxford English Dictionary"* (New York: HarperCollins, 1998), 239–40.

A bibliographic essay should be succinct—certainly not more than a few pages long—or readers may not be able to find the citations they want, even if the essay is divided by chapter or by theme. If a bibliographical essay is used, full citations should probably be given in the notes.

An annotated bibliography can be helpful in books intended for students. In this case, each entry in the bibliography is described in a phrase or two:

> Canfora, Luciano. *The Vanished Library: A Wonder of the Ancient World* (Berkeley and Los Angeles: University of California Press, 1989). A scholarly evocation of the history of the Ptolemaic library in Alexandria written as a mystery story.[4]

THE AUTHOR-DATE REFERENCE SYSTEM

An alternative to notes is the author-date reference system, which once was used primarily in the sciences but which has spread to the social sciences and even the humanities. One advantage of this system is its brevity; compared to the endnote system, it is quite a space-saver. Another advantage is clarity: readers familiar with the field will not have to turn to the back of the book to know whose work is being cited in a particular paragraph. That said, the author-date system tends to be less elegant and less versatile than the endnote system. Parenthetical references are ill suited to scholarly works that typically cite multiple sources at a single point in the text. Even short parenthetical citations can distract

---

4. Thomas R. Martin, *Ancient Greece: From Prehistoric to Hellenistic Times* (New Haven: Yale University Press, 2000), 237.

readers, so author-date citations may not be the best choice for books aimed at the elusive "general reader." If many of your sources are not easily identifiable by author and date (say, if the sources have no "author" per se), then this system should be avoided.

The mechanics of the author-date system are detailed in *The Chicago Manual of Style*. Here is how my example looks when this system is used:

> Most network users agree that writing styles are somehow transformed by the computer. In a survey by Ruth Ryan (1992), 95 percent of respondents "indicated they had encountered differences in communication using computer-mediated communication as opposed to face-to-face or traditional print methods." According to Bay Area Women in Telecommunications, however, in 1993 only 10 to 15 percent of the users on many computer systems were women (Truong 1993). Why? Possibly because much technology is designed by and for men (Smith and Balka 1988). Although Sherry Turkle and Seymour Papert (1990, 132) believe that "discrimination in the computer culture . . . is determined not by rules that keep people out but by ways of thinking that make them reluctant to join in," Paul Edwards (1995) maintains that computers are built to resist women's efforts to "make friends" with them.

In the author-date system, a reference list is mandatory. It includes all of the sources mentioned in the text, and only those sources. There are no exceptions. (This rule does not apply to bibliographies used with the humanities system.) The reference list for my example might look like this:

Edwards, Paul N. 1995. "From 'Impact' to Social Process: Computers in Society and Culture." In *Handbook of Science and Technology Studies*, edited by Sheila Jasanoff, Gerald E. Markle, James C. Peterson, and Trevor Pinch. Thousand Oaks, Calif.: Sage Publications.

Ryan, Ruth. 1992. "International Connectivity: A Survey of Attitudes about Cultural and National Differences Encountered in Computer-Mediated Communication." *Online Chronicle of Distance Education and Communication* 6, no. 1. http://www.eff.org/Net_culture/Infotopia/culture_and_comp_mediation.paper.

Smith, Judy, and Ellen Balka. 1988. "Chatting on a Feminist Computer Network." In *Technology and Women's Voices: Keeping in Touch*, edited by Cheris Kramarae. New York: Routledge and Kegan Paul.

Truong, Hoai-An. 1993. "Gender Issues in Online Communications." Version 4.3, with additional writing and editing by Gail Williams, Judi Clark, and Anna Couey, in conjunction with members of Bay Area Women in Telecommunications. http://www.cpsr.org/cpsr/gender/bawit.cfp93.

Turkle, Sherry, and Seymour Papert. 1990. "Epistemological Pluralism: Styles and Voices within the Computer Culture." *Signs: Journal of Women in Culture and Society* 16, no. 1: 128–155.

When revising a thesis that uses the author-date system, get rid of long strings of names and dates in the text. Not only do such chains highlight the unfortunate clunkiness of the system, but they do the reader no favors. Pick the one or two most authoritative, relevant, and useful sources, and eliminate the others from both text and reference list.

Notes can be used in combination with the author-date system. In that case, back-of-book or foot-of-page notes are used—

sparingly—to illuminate or amplify a point made in the text. Citations are given in author-date form regardless of whether they appear in the text or in a note. The reference list includes works cited in text and notes. This hybrid gives the author-date format a little more flexibility but poses the risk of weighing down the book with unnecessary notes.

A different combination of the notes and author-date systems dispenses with in-text citations altogether and uses note superscripts instead. In the end-of-book notes, no full citations are given, just author-date forms. Although this system makes for a clean page (as the endnote system does), you lose the main advantages of the author-date system: the citations are no longer right in front of you as you read the text, and you don't save as much space because each note must take up at least one entire line.

OTHER SYSTEMS OF DOCUMENTATION

For books that are aimed at a wide audience, neither the endnote system nor the author-date system may be ideal. Although few revised dissertations truly appeal to the so-called general reader, a less obtrusive system of documentation may be worth considering if yours is one of those few.

One option is the unnumbered-note system, consisting of endnotes that are not keyed to superscripts in the text. The text reads cleanly, uninterrupted by note numbers. In the back of the book, the notes are keyed to a page number and an introductory phrase:

> [page] 4   "The picture that has emerged . . .": Bill Barol,
> "Men Aren't Her Only Problem," *Newsweek*, Nov.
> 23, 1987, p. 76.

4	Four-fifths of them . . . : Shere Hite, *Women and Love: A Cultural Revolution in Progress* (New York: Knopf, 1987), pp. 41–42.
5	The *Washington Post* even . . . : "Things Getting Worse for Hite," *San Francisco Chronicle*, Nov. 14, 1987, p. C9.
5	"Characteristically grandiose . . .": Claudia Wallis, "Back Off, Buddy," *Time*, Oct. 12, 1987, p. 68.
5	And Hite specifically . . . : Hite, *Women and Love*, pp. 774–78.[5]

This system is appropriate only when notes are few and far between—ideally limited to sources for material quoted in the text. For general-interest works that require heavier documentation (for example, a book with a controversial thesis contradicting previous research), unnumbered notes are frustrating in the extreme: a reader must guess whether a particular allegation is supported by a note and, upon turning to the back of the book, may well find that it isn't. Furthermore, the reader isn't the only one for whom this system is a chore: the editor cannot change a word in the text without ensuring that the corresponding introductory phrase in the note is changed too, lest the note become impossible to find. And once the book has been typeset and paginated, the typesetter must make a separate (potentially costly) pass to add the correct page number to each note.

Some of these pitfalls are avoided by an even less meticulous option: to include no documentation other than lists of sources, further readings, or bibliographical essays, either at the end of

---

5. Susan Faludi, *Backlash: The Undeclared War against American Women* (New York: Doubleday, 1991), 466.

each chapter or at the back of the book but gathered by chapter. This plan is not usually appropriate for a revised thesis but can be useful for certain books truly intended for a general audience— say, a nutrition manual for diabetics or a field guide to birds—or for a book designed primarily as a textbook.

Yet another system of documentation, sometimes called the citation-sequence system, is often used in journals, especially in the natural and social sciences. It involves notes keyed to a numbered reference list. References are organized in the order in which they appear: reference 1 is the first work cited, reference 2 the second, and so on. If more than one reference is cited in one place in the text, two note numbers appear there. A cited work is given the same number regardless of how many times it is mentioned. As a result, the superscript numbers almost invariably appear out of order after a page or so. This system is not workable in a book, mainly because the entire reference list—and all the notes—must be renumbered if one work is added or deleted during revision or later editing. Another disadvantage is that if the reference list is long, note numbers could reach three digits and result in awkward typography.

Finally, some authors and publishers have suggested that those who have trouble trimming their documentation might wish to make some or all of it available electronically, either on the Internet or on a CD-ROM. Scholars who want to do in-depth research, the argument goes, can refer to the Web site mentioned in the book or pop the CD into a handy drive. This plan is problematic for several reasons. One reason is obvious but probably temporary: the technology is relatively new and changing fast. At the moment, there is no guarantee that a particular Web site will still be in place several years after the book's publication, and CD-ROMs could soon be obsolete. Furthermore, some readers could lack either access to the technology or the know-how required to use it.

My second argument is more substantial: a book needs to be complete in itself. Some authors plan to include note super-scripts in the text but omit the notes from the book, instead choosing to post them on the Internet. Many readers and book reviewers, not to mention many publishers, object to that. The key components of a book must be part of the book, or it lacks integrity and authority. More sensible is the idea of putting an ancillary bibliography, appendixes, primary source documents, or tables on the Web—bearing in mind that these documents may not have the same permanence as the printed book. In that case, the Web site is completely separate from the printed book and may be cited as a reference, but readers of the book need not rely on it.

TABLES AND GRAPHS

Each table, chart, or graph in a book interrupts the flow of the text. The interruption is costly in terms of production expenses (a table is complicated and expensive to typeset, and a graph often carries extra printing costs) and costly also in terms of the reader's attention span. If the material covered in a table can be summa-rized in a sentence, or even a paragraph, then delete the table: it would take up more space than the verbal summary. For example, table 5.1 can be summarized as follows:

Table 5.1 *Incidence of Measles in Cadboro County*

Year	Measles Cases	Deaths
1850	52	35
1900	17	6
1950	2	0

In 1850 in Cadboro County, 52 people came down with measles, and two-thirds of them died. In 1900 only 17 people got measles, and only 6 of them died. By 1950 there were only 2 cases and no deaths.

The table takes up just as much space as the summary, looks more technical, and doesn't highlight what is important about the data.

When should a table or graph be retained? The answer is, when it is the most efficient way to present a large amount of information and when the information is central to the argument (table 5.2 is an example of a table that works). If the information is not central to the argument, then the data should be deleted from the book or, at the very least, relegated to an appendix. An appendix is a good place for essential data supporting your conclusions, thus leaving the text free for the presentation and explanation of those conclusions. But if the data are not essential—because scholars can reconstruct them, because they are available elsewhere, or because they are not central to the argument—then it's best to leave out that material entirely.

The fewer tables in the book, the better. Several similar tables (tables 5.3, 5.4, and 5.5) can easily be combined into a single concise one (table 5.6).

Table 5.2 *Mortality Trends in Cadboro County*

Year	All Causes	Cancer		Heart Disease		Infectious Diseases	
		N	%	N	%	N	%
1900	523	83	16	133	25	85	16
1910	417	95	23	157	38	65	16
1920	776	102	13	195	25	70	9
1930	879	320	36	210	24	53	6
1940	853	401	47	226	26	42	5
1950	920	543	59	213	23	23	3

Table 5.3 *Incidence of Three Diseases in Cadboro County*

Year	Measles Cases	Mumps Cases	Influenza Cases
1850	52	60	63
1900	17	35	77
1950	2	7	67

Table 5.4 *Incidence of Three Diseases in Sinclair County*

	Measles Cases	Mumps Cases	Influenza Cases
1850	7	3	15
1900	8	8	12
1950	0	0	50

Table 5.5 *Incidence of Three Diseases in Parkwood County*

	Measles Cases	Mumps Cases	Influenza Cases
1850	76	0	75
1900	25	0	90
1950	0	0	72

Table 5.6 *Incidence of Disease in Three Counties*

	Cadboro County	Sinclair County	Parkwood County
1850			
Measles	52	7	76
Mumps	60	3	0
Influenza	63	15	75
1900			
Measles	17	8	25
Mumps	35	8	0
Influenza	77	12	90
1950			
Measles	2	0	0
Mumps	7	0	0
Influenza	67	50	72

A table can contain too much information as well as too little. If it has more than five or six columns, it may be too wide to fit in the book without being turned sideways, which is awkward for readers. A wide table may work better if the columns are made into rows. Another option is to delete a column or two.

If one complex table is referred to over a span of several

printed pages, readers will tire of flipping back to it. In that case, consider breaking the long table into two smaller ones. The aim is to make a wealth of information available to the reader in the most effective and succinct way.

Once you have decided which tables and graphs to retain (if any), look at how they are discussed in the text. Of course, each table or graph must be relevant to the text and should be mentioned. But do not repeat or describe the data found in the table. Instead, analyze and interpret the information. What are its implications? How does it fit into the argument? What conclusions can be drawn from it?

Graphs present their own issues. They can be used to show, at a glance, the conclusions or trends that you have gleaned from tabular material, but they, even more than tables, can often be summarized in a sentence or two. For example, figure 5.1 can be summarized as follows:

> The incidence of measles and mumps in Cadboro County
> declined steadily between 1850 and 1950, but the number of
> flu cases remained almost constant.

If you determine that a graph (or, even more rarely, a pie chart) is not wasted space but truly the most efficient way to make your point, make sure that it is clear and will reproduce well. In a bar graph, do not use five different shades of gray, which may all look the same once the book is printed, and avoid busy patterns that confuse the eye. Be sure that each bar is distinguishable at a glance (figure 5.2).

Bear in mind that tables, charts, and graphs make a book look technical. If you wish to attract a wide audience or make your

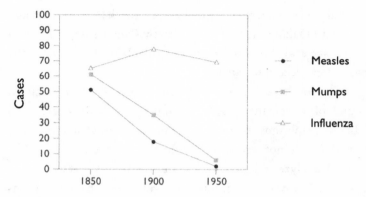

Figure 5.1   Incidence of Three Diseases in Cadboro County, Line Graph

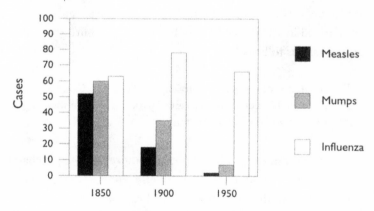

Figure 5.2   Incidence of Three Diseases in Cadboro County, Bar Graph

book appeal to nonspecialist readers, stick to words whenever possible.

When you write a dissertation, your scholarship, your methodology, and your research are all out in the open for readers to appraise. By contrast, when you write a book, that scholarly foundation should be the iceberg of which your book is merely the visible tip.

Have your ideal readers in mind as you revise. What will they want to learn? What would they find offputting, extraneous, or boring? Any writer, not just those revising a thesis, would do well to take John Ruskin's advice: "Say all you have to say in the fewest possible words, or your reader will be sure to skip them; and in the plainest possible words or he will certainly misunderstand them."

PART II

DISCIPLINARY VARIATIONS

6

CAUGHT IN THE MIDDLE

THE HUMANITIES

Jennifer Crewe

In recent years it has become more and more difficult for a scholar to publish a specialized monograph in the humanities. At the very moment when administrators are increasing the publication requirements for tenure and promotion, university presses are cutting back in these fields because so many of the books—particularly revised dissertations by unknown scholars—do not sell enough copies to earn back the costs of publication. So junior scholars are caught in the middle—trying to publish one, two, and sometimes even three books before they come up for tenure, only to find rejection letters in the inbox at the end of the day. This crisis—it's not too strong a word—is being addressed by the scholarly associations in some disciplines, such as history and literature. I hope that administrators will get the message and change tenure requirements and that they will consider journal articles and peer-reviewed electronic publication to be acceptable and even preferable in some cases to book publication. But in the meantime humanities scholars must live with an ever-tightening market and write their books for the broadest possible audience.

In this chapter I will present one publisher's view of the best way to write and present your book to a prospective publisher.

A DISSERTATION IS NOT A BOOK

You've heard the following advice before, no doubt, but it is worth repeating. Once the dissertation is finished you'll feel compelled to publish it right away. Resist this urge. The initial revision of your manuscript should be attempted only after you have put it aside and not looked at it for at least several months, and after you have reread it with the eyes of a reader who has never heard of you or your committee. I sometimes still receive manuscripts with the dissertation cover page still on top ("submitted in partial fulfillment of the requirements . . ."), and that tells me that the author has just successfully defended the dissertation and sent it off to me without giving a thought to the eventual book's true audience. Most editors at university presses would not even send the manuscript out for review at this stage. Even if the topic is compelling and the editor is interested, chances are that reviewers (if the manuscript is sent out for review) will point out that a considerable amount of revision is necessary before the manuscript is really a book, and the reviews may not be favorable enough for the editor to proceed. Of course there are exceptions—occasionally a dissertation is written by someone with prior journalistic experience, or by someone who has written other books, or by someone who is an extraordinarily mature writer. But usually a dissertation is written by someone who has spent too many years as an apprentice and is anxious to get a job.

As the authors of earlier chapters have noted, the audience for a dissertation usually consists of four or five people, the student's doctoral committee. The author has written it to prove that he or she has done the appropriate research, performed convincing analysis, come up with original conclusions, and put it all together in a coherent narrative, dutifully addressing the various committee members' particular interests. A book, by contrast, should be written for a wider audience of people interested in your topic. This audience will include scholars and graduate students who are working in your specific area of research, or generally in the field addressed in your book, and even—if you're lucky, and the book is well written and on a fairly broad topic or one of current interest among the media—some educated general readers. The audience will also include reviewers of your book, both before and after it is published. These readers do not need an exhaustive literature review, hundreds of footnotes to justify everything you say, or lengthy and tedious refutations of work by scholars who have come before you. Your audience will not appreciate your showing how well you can use jargon—in most cases they will appreciate your avoidance of specialized language.

Often, however, revising your dissertation is not just a matter of removing the literature review, trimming the notes, and toning down the jargon. A dissertation must in many cases be reconceptualized and expanded in scope before it can become a successful—or even a publishable—book.

But first, why not consider whether you really want to put all that work into a dissertation you've already spent years writing and revising and have finally defended? Are you sick of the topic? If so, your style will suffer. Are you worried the book will become dated or no longer fashionable in two to three years' time? In either case I would recommend carving up the dissertation to produce one or two or three excellent scholarly articles, and then putting it aside and coming up with a new book topic, one that may grow naturally out of the research you did for the dissertation but that is free of the constraints of writing for your committee. The book you produce will no doubt be a more mature and more readable work than the revised dissertation would have been.

ARTICLES OR A BOOK?

Many of the book abstracts and manuscripts that come across my desk are really overblown scholarly articles. Indeed, many of the scholarly monographs published recently in humanities fields such as literary and cultural studies, film, and religion could have been articles, but because of the pressure to publish books for tenure, their authors have been forced to pad them. And many scholarly books these days are nothing more than a collection of articles. I had lunch the other day with an author who told me that all of his chapters were completed in draft form. Now all he had to do was "find the glue to stick them together." Most significant and memorable books in the humanities are written after—not before—the author has a notion of what the overarching message will be, and the chapters flow naturally from one to the other as the author builds the argument. My hunch is that this author was trying to make a book out of related but basically disparate articles, many of them previously published in journals. Scholars must realize that, because library budgets are so limited, many librarians won't purchase a book if they already own most of its contents in the form of articles in journals they subscribe to. Book publishers are aware of this and are leery of taking on a book if most of its contents have already been published.

When deciding whether to turn your dissertation into a book or publish it as one or more articles, ask yourself this: Could your core idea be conveyed succinctly and perhaps more powerfully in fifty pages, or do you really need two hundred? Publishing a couple of articles from the book has a number of advantages. First, you don't have to worry as much about rewriting for a broader audience. Second, you can publish the essential conclusions from your dissertation relatively quickly, without having to spend a year or more adding to and revising the manuscript and then submitting it for publication. Finally, if you are ready to move on to another project, you will be able to turn to it more quickly, and the new project can be written from the beginning as a book for a larger audience.

TOPIC

BREADTH. Whether you decide to make a book out of your dissertation or embark on a wholly new project, if you want to publish it eventually as a book you have to first consider your topic. Is it really a book topic? If the topic is going to be of interest only to you and the twenty other people who care passionately about your subfield, it is more suited to an article or series of articles that will reach subscribers to a journal who might otherwise not read your material and who wouldn't be likely to buy your book. If on the other hand your topic is sufficiently broad to attract readers beyond your subfield and even beyond your own discipline, and if it contains a sustained argument, it is more suited to book form.

INTERDISCIPLINARITY—GOOD OR BAD? Many people think that if their topic is interdisciplinary, their publisher will be pleased because the book will interest more people. That *can* be true, but it is usually true *only* if the author is well known in both (or all) fields addressed in the book. I once published a book whose author was known (that is, she presented papers at conferences and published in the relevant journals) in three disciplines: literary studies, film, and Asian studies. Her book really did sell well in all three disciplines. However, an author who has a Ph.D. in English but who is simply using historical methods or citing many history sources is probably not going to be known to historians. What is more, his book is probably not going to be purchased by historians, who, in my experience, generally do not consider literary scholars to have had the proper training to write history. Many authors who dabble in other fields claim that their book will be purchased by scholars in those fields, but it usually doesn't happen.

THE PERILS OF TRENDY TOPICS. If you are going to choose a topic that is very trendy today, remember that by the time you have finished your book—at least several years from now—it may be yesterday's news and extremely difficult to publish. And remember that it takes almost a year from the time of acceptance of a manuscript to the time you actually hold the first copy in your hands. A few years ago the words *race, class,* and *gender* graced the title or subtitle of almost four hundred submissions I received in a single year in literary studies. Some of these scholars even seemed to have forced the consideration of race or class into a book that actually had a largely different focus. A couple of years later *postcoloniality* was the term in the vast majority of titles of books submitted to me in this field. Ten years before that, almost every submission had a portion of a word in the title in parentheses or featured a slash or two. Punctuation within a word in a title was very popular. As you can imagine, these books all sound alike to an editor after the first dozen or so. Our eyes glaze over and we're inclined to reject the book right away. We simply can't afford to publish something that is so like every other book in the field that it won't get any attention. It is far better to choose a topic that you think will have some staying power than to ride the wave of fashion. Of course, fashion cannot be ignored entirely or your book could seem unexciting or out of date to a prospective employer or publisher.

AUDIENCE

Scholars often assume that university presses exist to serve them and that it is the presses' duty to publish anything that fits their list and reviews well. The fact is, university presses do consider it their mission to publish important new scholarly work, but the manuscript has to have a sufficient and identifiable audience. If not enough scholars and librarians will pay for the book, the university press may find it impossible to take on because the costs of publication will far outweigh the anticipated sales revenue.

As you are writing, keep your audience in mind. As I mentioned earlier, the audience for your book is not the same (we hope) as the tiny audience for your dissertation. Hundreds of books are published each year in each field. Readers can no longer keep up with all the publications and are making choices. If the book seems as though it will be a chore to wade through, or is so focused on one specific topic that it doesn't seem directly applicable to their own area of research, they won't buy it. Authors invariably overestimate the number of people who will actually buy their book. It's important to write for as broad an audience as possible, clearly, with a minimum of academic jargon, so that you can cast your net wide.

WRITING STYLE

Publishers pay a lot of attention to an author's writing style. That is because if the book is written in an accessible, inviting manner it could mean a big difference in the size of the book's audience. I have frequently attended an editorial meeting and heard the marketing director say that the topic of the book under discussion sounded great and she thought the book could reach a general audience. But later, after the editor sent her a copy of the manuscript to read, she retracted her initial enthusiasm, saying that the prose was impenetrable and only specialists would buy the book. Most authors feel that they are good writers, so criticism of this sort is hard to take. In addition, many scholarly authors in the humanities feel that there is no avoiding academic jargon and endless dense sentences if they are to be taken seriously in their field. This is a shame because once you start writing that way it's extremely difficult to change. An author of mine told me once, "Okay, now that I've written two books for specialists in my field, I'm ready to write for the educated general reader." But what he sent me was stiff, stilted, and oddly dumbed down. He had no notion of how to say what he wanted to say clearly but not simplistically.

Ask a friend who is a scholar in a different field, or a relative or someone you believe to be an educated general reader, to read your chapters as you write them and to flag anything that seems confusing or unclear. This is a good way to draw you out of the habit of writing for a thesis committee and into the habit of writing for a wider world.

TITLE

The choice of a title for your manuscript is extremely important. I don't just mean the final title that appears on your printed book, which may end up being quite different from the one that graced your submission. The first thing the acquiring editor looks at when you send a query letter is your book title. Some of us, out of habit or to save time or both, tend to ignore all other prose in the letter and go to the title first. If the title is appealing, we'll read the letter carefully. If the title indicates that the book is in a field or subfield that doesn't relate in any way to the publishing program at our press, we turn the book down right away. If the title is endless and jargon filled, we assume the book is too. If the title is so vague that it doesn't convey much of anything about the book, it nevertheless conveys to the editor that there may be a problem. The title can be metaphorical as long as the subtitle, or the sentence immediately following the title, explains clearly what the book is about.

INTRODUCTION AND FIRST CHAPTER

If the editor gets beyond the cover letter, she will read the introduction, or first chapter, if that's what the author sent. These first few pages are crucial. If they are engaging and catch the editor's interest, they've done their job. This is no place for an exhaustive literature review or a boring recitation of everything your book is *not* going to address. This is the place where you clearly state the objectives of your book and draw the reader in. An anecdote or personal note can be helpful here. The introduction should be clearly structured and clearly written and should lay the groundwork for what is to come. If the book is published and reviewed, this is the section the reviewers will read first, and probably most carefully; reviewers will probably quote from it. And this is the section that browsers in the store will look at when they are deciding whether to purchase the book. Likewise, the opening of every chapter should be clear and inviting. The editor and book reviewer will pay most attention to these sections.

THE MAIN BODY OF THE TEXT

REPETITION. Go through your manuscript carefully before you send it to an editor to be sure that you are not repeating yourself from chapter to chapter or even within chapters. It is very common, in a book that has been written over a long period of time, to encounter such repetitions. The author doesn't see them any more!

EXCESSIVE QUOTATION. Lengthy quotations from the scholars who have come before you in your field may be flattering to them and appropriate in a dissertation, but they're downright annoying in a book. Quotation is more effective when it's used briefly (in other words, avoid long block quotations) and only when necessary.

CONCLUSION. Avoid just ending your manuscript when your final case study or final chapter comes to a close. Bring the reader back around to your main points by summarizing them in a brief conclusion. This is also the place where you can point forward—to your next book, perhaps, or show where future work could be done to carry on this particular argument. After the introduction and table of contents, many acquiring editors turn to the conclusion when they are trying to determine whether to consider the manuscript for publication.

LENGTH. Generally speaking, the longer the book the more expensive it is to produce and the higher the price tag the publisher must place on it. The higher the price tag, the smaller the audience. Libraries as well as individuals are very cautious about their spending on books, particularly in the humanities. Scientists often have research budgets, a portion of which is specifically set aside for the purchase of books. Alas, most humanists have no such luxury, and the money they spend on books comes out of their own pockets. I have seen scholars spend fifteen minutes in a publishers' booth at a conference, reading through the section of a book they're interested in, even taking a few notes, and then putting the book back on the shelf and leaving, without giving a thought to purchasing it. So please give some thought to length when you are writing your book.

How long is too long? Some editors start to wince only when they think a book will exceed four hundred printed pages—that is, more than about 160,000 words (unless the book is a reference work or a textbook that requires a certain coverage). But even a monograph much longer than 120,000 words (or about three hundred book pages), including notes and bibliography, can be a difficult book to publish and to sell. Don't try to cram as many words on a page as possible by picking one of those nifty fonts that takes up less space so that the manuscript you submit *seems* shorter than it is. Editors don't even talk about manuscript pages any more because they can be so deceptive. Tell the editor how many words your manuscript contains, including notes and bibliography. If you suspect it may be too long and know that you can easily make some cuts, tell the editor that as well.

ILLUSTRATIONS. Illustrations can be a strong selling feature as long as they are interesting, pertinent to the argument, and readable when reduced to about a third of a book page in black and white. Most editors will welcome them—as long as there are not too many. In my experience, up to about twenty-five black-and-white illustrations will not add significantly to the cost of the book and will enhance its salability. A book with fifty or more illustrations can be quite costly to produce, but in some cases a large number may be necessary. The editor will have to factor in the cost of the illustrations in determining whether the press can afford to publish the book. You should not demand up front that the editor include each of your two hundred photos. Showing that you can be flexible will go a long way to endearing yourself to your editor. If you know of a source of funding to help offset the press's production costs, the editor will be grateful.

BACK MATTER

ENDNOTES. Notes are helpful embellishments to the text or provide the reader with sources indicating where you found your information. The main purpose of the notes is *not* to show off how much you've read. That may be acceptable at the dissertation stage, perhaps, but your book should not be burdened with excessive notes. If you hope for a general readership, hold the notes to essential information.

BIBLIOGRAPHY. Likewise, a bibliography is a useful tool, but overkill—for example, a twenty-page bibliography with several subsections—is not a good idea unless you are writing a reference book or a sourcebook.

APPENDIXES. These should be included only if absolutely necessary. If the manuscript is too long, your editor will ask you to remove them. Consider putting them on a Web site that the press can link to from its own Web page announcing your book.

CHOICE OF A PUBLISHER

Once you have a manuscript that is written for a broad community of peers and beyond, how do you go about getting it published?

First look at similar books in your own field that have been published in the last two years. Who published them? Visit these publishers' Web sites. Would your book really fit in with the other offerings of these presses? Find out the name of the editor who handles your field. Find out whether she accepts e-mail queries or would prefer to receive an inquiry by mail. Often this information is on the site.

Go to the exhibit area during your field's annual meeting and look at the offerings of particular presses you're interested in. You can talk to the editor there, but make it brief: "Would you be interested in . . ." and a brief sentence to describe your book is enough. Editors are very busy and are often on overload at these meetings. A fifteen-minute description of Chapter 5 won't endear you to the editor.

PRESENTATION TO THE PUBLISHER

Once you've chosen the optimal press, send a brief (one-page) cover letter or e-mail it to the appropriate editor. This letter should, in one or two short paragraphs, describe the book. A somewhat longer abstract and table of contents can accompany the letter. The ability to summarize a manuscript clearly, succinctly, and in an interesting manner will help make your book stand out from the crowd. An inability to describe your book in one paragraph is a red flag for the editor; it speaks volumes about the writer. I once considered a submission by someone who came highly recommended to me by one of my authors. When my author described his friend's book, it sounded interesting. But the writer's cover letter to me was so abstruse that I couldn't figure out what the writer was going to argue in his book. It was four single-spaced pages long. I finally asked him to please e-mail me a one-paragraph description of the book. Days passed. A week later he sent me a somewhat whittled-down two-page description. He was incapable of doing what I'd asked. That told me that I could never hope to describe the book succinctly and accurately to my colleagues and that our copywriter would never be able to distill it for our catalog and on the jacket copy. I turned the book down.

Your letter should also describe the book's "true market" or, in other words: Who do you think will actually fork over some hard-earned cash to purchase your book? Don't be tempted to say that scholars in eighteen fields will be interested in your book—the editor won't believe it. Be realistic. Briefly compare the book with one or two recent books in the field, preferably well-known ones, and explain how yours fits into the dialogue and what is so important about your book. You could include a table of contents and possibly the introduction, but don't deluge the editor with material. If your book has true course adoption potential (not just that you and your best friend will assign it to a graduate seminar), mention that possibility, and name the specific courses and level.

SUBSIDIES

An editor will always welcome news of a possible subsidy for your book. If your university has a grant program to help defray the cost of photographs, permissions, or a four-color jacket, or just to offset plant and printing costs, let your editor know. Or if your research was funded by a foundation that also has a book subsidy program, let the editor know. It costs a lot to publish a book—much more, in some cases, than the publisher can hope to recoup through sales. Any subsidy will help your publisher, and in some cases a subsidy will allow the publisher to accept the book and sell it for a price that is reasonable. Editors are often torn about particular books if they look interesting but might lose money. Most of us were drawn to scholarly publishing because we believe in the ideal of publishing excellent work even if it doesn't have a large audience. But we know that if the press we work for is to survive, and if we are to keep our jobs, we must be fiscally responsible as well. In most cases we simply cannot accept a book that we and our colleagues know will not earn back its costs.

EDITORS ARE BUSY PEOPLE

If you haven't had a response to your query letter a month after you've sent it, it's perfectly acceptable to send a follow-up. Chances are, the editor hasn't yet had a chance to read it or has read it quickly and put it aside for a more careful look. Don't be afraid to send a follow-up query if more than a month has gone by. Once in a while a proposal goes astray and the editor isn't even aware that you sent it, and if you wait six months to find this out, you've wasted valuable time.

ETIQUETTE

I hope I will not be met with astonishment, or irritation, if I conclude this chapter with a brief word about manners. It's amazing how many scholars, under the tremendous stress of trying to publish their books in a hurry, become rude to their potential publishers. Frequently they have finished the manuscript at the nth hour and need a response from the publisher yesterday in order to come up for tenure or promotion. The editor has many hurdles to jump before she can offer you a contract, and she is often dependent upon reviewers who may or may not meet their deadlines. Make it clear that you would like an answer by a certain date, bearing in mind that about two months is probably the shortest time in which you could receive an answer. Once your book is approved, don't assume you know more about publishing than your editor does. A few conversations with friends and acquaintances who have published books does not equal the years of daily publishing experience your editor has to draw on.

Make suggestions, not demands. Take no for an answer. If your editor has just told you the decision has been made to publish your book in hardcover only, or that you can include only half the photos you wanted to include, or that the book can't possibly be produced in six months, in time for it to be eligible for a particular prize or displayed at a convention, it's fine to find out why the decision has been made and to plead your case. But don't be relentless in your quest to change her mind. Decisions such as these are made by several people in the company and are not only in her hands. What's more, there are usually very good reasons behind them. Perhaps most important, keep in mind that she is your advocate—if you alienate your editor, you've lost your closest ally in the company. If you alienate your editor's colleagues, you've caused a problem, both for your book and for your editor in house.

GOOD LUCK!

These are difficult times in scholarly publishing, and the humanities are being hit particularly hard. But it's not a hopeless task to publish your book. Thousands of scholarly books in the humanities are published each year. Chances are, yours will be one of them.

7

PUTTING PASSION INTO SOCIAL SCIENCE

Peter J. Dougherty and Charles T. Myers

On a recent visit to a used book dealer on Nassau Street in Princeton, New Jersey, we listened to the proprietor intone a deadpan, even deadly, comment: that no book published in the field of politics in the past decade is worth a plugged nickel on the used book market. This earnest dealer, who pays the rent by playing the spread between the price at which he buys used books and that at which he can resell them, had essentially given up political science—and, we think fair to say, large portions of other social science fields such as geography, sociology, anthropology, economic history, and psychology—for lost. As social science editors who have read a few too many book proposals in which the authors succeed only in draining the life out of potentially vibrant and important questions, we can understand why. We have seen proposals for books on (to name one topic) ethnic conflict in which the subject is reduced to a methodological means of testing conflicting theories of international relations, leaving only the barest hint that tens of thousands of people have died as the result of the ethnic hostilities in question.

Our local bookseller's lament, which most intellectuals would regard as a sad commentary on the state of literary culture, sounds even more depressing to social science editors. Like our friend, we make our living in books. We publish some of the very social science books that promise with such chilly predictability to be commercially dead on arrival in the market. Our authors, many of them young social scientists embarking on careers in political science or sociology or geography or economic history, build their reputations on these same books. Moreover, these authors use their books to communicate ideas vital to their colleagues, critics, and students and to enlarge society's store of self-knowledge.

Our publishing forebears tell us that things were different for social science books in the good old days of fatter social science research grants and more bountiful library budgets. Back then scholarly publishers could shift enough copies of most books to cover costs, make a few bucks, keep authors and colleagues happy, and keep the wolf from the door. Maybe so. But is there any evidence that even in those good old days the additional books sold to libraries were read by more people than those of today? These anxieties raise fundamental questions as to what steps an aspiring social scientist needs to take to get the most out of the exhausting effort put into researching a dissertation and revising it into a book on which great hopes ride.

How do we move forward? How do we counsel our authors and prospective authors to prepare their books, including revised dissertations, the main building blocks of knowledge in most social sciences, for publication? And how do we publish these books once they arrive, manila wrapped, in our offices? As we hope to convey in this chapter, the key to successful publication in social science is a commitment on the part of authors and authors-to-be to *core ideas* and to a mastery of the means of bringing these core ideas alive. As great social science books of the past have proved, authors have to evince some passion for their ideas—and evoke some passion in their readers—for their books to enjoy true success. This commitment begins in the conception of a compelling first chapter, a crisp proposal, and eventually a strong manuscript, attractive to readers, reviewers, and foreign co-publishers alike. Abetting this goal is the author's understanding of the context in which the book will be published: the social science editor's place in identifying and selecting books for publication, the senior scholar or series editor's part in facilitating publication, and the editor's role in leveraging the publisher's internal resources to get the book published well.

WEIRD SCIENCE: BEYOND THE BASICS

Seven chapters deep into a book on the craft of dissertation revision, we are merely repeating dogma to insist that there is a real difference between a dissertation and a book and that this difference must be bridged if a new author is to successfully write a good book. The fundamental things apply: Think about your ideal intended reader. Adopt a chapter structure that generates some tension and engages this reader even as a good map tantalizes the prospective traveler. State the basic argument in its entirety at the book's beginning, not at its end. Modulate the level of discourse throughout the book. Use rich, telling examples. Employ an evocative though accurate title and strong chapter titles. End the book on a prospective note indicating the direction of future research.

All of these measures matter greatly and yet somehow fail to get at the heart of the challenge of successful book writing in *social science*. A clue to the problem lies in the rather oxymoronic term *social science* itself. Good political science or geography bears many of the marks of scientific method, language, and structure. Neoclassical economics has been described (harshly, in our view) as physics with money. These characteristics are, in some measure, the necessary machinery of the scientific study of social phenomena. The problem is that social science all too often reads like machinery. In translating a social science dissertation into a book, the first and most important lesson is to frame the study in such a way that readers—whom we take to be a reasonably broad audience of scholars and graduate students but certainly not the "educated general reader," whoever he or she is—can engage and savor the basic argument without having to divine a specialized scientific language.

Social science books, if they are to succeed, must be couched in the larger intellectual and social discourse: in the "human conversation," to use a phrase made popular by the economic historian Deirdre McCloskey. This conversation is a matter of stories, not A-primes, betas, and repeated games. Social science authors have to be able to tell good stories about their A-primes and betas and repeated games to engage readers and make their books come alive. Remember that the subject of social science is human behavior: a subject of intense and enduring interest to readers in all places and at all times. Too often social scientists fail to capture the broader human implications of their topics in their books. As a result, it is not unusual for us to find ourselves presenting projects to our editorial board, only to hear a board member from an unrelated discipline say, "I already knew that." Hence, we proffer our first bit of advice: the Great Introductory Chapter Maxim. Write as compelling a first chapter as you can—one that animates your core idea, brings it to life, and situates it in the reader's experience. The better the takeoff, the better the trip.

GETTING STARTED

A compelling introductory chapter will inform and inspire the rest of your book. Draft a first chapter your readers will learn from and love and return to for the sake of learning more. This tactic constitutes a vital step toward converting your social science dissertation into a good book. What holds true for revised dissertations as a matter of fact holds true for all scholarly books, but the sad truth is that some social science authors never learn this lesson, which is partly why literary social science has earned its Transylvanian reputation. How, asks the eager young author, does one write a great introductory chapter? The best advice we can offer is to read, study, and master some of the truly great ones.

One of us (Dougherty), who has labored as an editor in the fields of sociology and economics for a generation, likes to direct his authors—first-timers and veterans alike—to the first chapter of the 1948 classic work *Social Theory and Social Structure,* by the late sociologist Robert K. Merton. This book is not a revised dissertation but a collection of scholarly essays that has sold hundreds of thousands of copies since its original publication and is still very much in print (in hardback only!) a half-century on. Merton's introductory chapter to his book is like an appetizer to a hearty and elegant meal. He revels in his subject, conveys the excitement of it, and provokes the reader's interest by placing the subject in the broadest historical and intellectual contexts. Merton's field, the sociology of science, emerges as a great and exciting scholarly adventure, a trip around the world, even to the uninitiated reader. Merton is a model for the ages, but one model is not enough. The serious social science author-to-be needs a sampler of great first chapters for inspiration. But the challenge of revising your dissertation doesn't stop there.

AUDIENCE IS EVERYTHING

In social science, not all potential topics lend themselves equally well to books. A certain topic may be the basis for a good social science dissertation but not an equally promising foundation for a good book. Such a topic may be of only narrow interest or may be too technical, foreclosing the possibility of an audience of sufficient size to support a book. For example, one senior scholar in international relations argues that the field's galloping technical sophistication has placed it beyond the grasp of much of the profession. The same could be said these days of other fields, from economic history through historical geography. Increasing mathematical complexity is now a real challenge in the publication of social science books. It requires not only that authors write compelling first chapters that can be read and savored by the majority of intended readers but also that those authors keep their readers engaged throughout their books.

For example, a game-theoretic treatment of the operations of central European parliaments that makes for a prize-winning dissertation might suffer as a book from the limited overlap between the set of people who read game theory and the set of people who care about the parliaments of central Europe. A successful scholarly book should of course answer a question of interest to a specific community of professional readers. But even books of interest primarily to professional political scientists must demonstrate why their arguments are important enough to justify someone's actually *buying a book* instead of merely reading journal articles. This requires constant attention to presentation.

If your topic is of interest to a large enough audience of readers, you have to think about how to explain your contribution in a way readers can understand. Keep the audience in mind constantly as you revise. State the broader question and offer your answers up front; be bold in stating your argument. Constantly consider how you present your argument so that you effectively communicate core ideas and do not simply demonstrate your methodological or theoretical virtuosity—you have already done that in the dissertation. Place the explanation of your methodology in an appendix. Do not fall back on the crutch of specialized language if you can use plain English to make your case. As each of us has said to authors from time to time, we are not asking that you dumb down your book; we are asking you to work harder at conveying core ideas and arguments.

Many social scientists want to reach a policy audience. Most of the proposals one of us (Myers) receives in political science include a sentence that must automatically flow from the computers of political scientists about the policy relevance of the study. Yet most will fail in this attempt because they either do not ask the question that real policy makers ask or do not use the language that policy makers or their staff speak. There are exceptions: one thinks of works such as Eric Redman's classic *The Dance of Legislation* as models of the crossover policy genre.

So what goes for the first chapter also goes for the rest of the book. Revise with respect for the reader and you will increase your chances of reaching the broadest possible market. Clear exposition matters. Social science editors do turn down books because of bad writing. We edit but we do not salvage. Manuscript length and typographical complexity matter as well. Longer books are priced higher, are often harder to get produced and reviewed, and are extremely difficult to have translated. Foreign publishers place a premium on shorter books that can be translated relatively quickly and cheaply. If the number of tables or illustrations is excessive, that can give an otherwise enthusiastic editor pause.

WRITE A GREAT BOOK PROPOSAL

Social science editors start their assessments with book proposals and see hundreds of them per year. Proposals (or prospectuses, as they are sometimes known) should be four to five double-spaced pages long, should state the thesis and describe the contribution of the book, should outline the argument and the evidence, should place the book in its proper intellectual and literary context, should describe the audience for the book, and should provide details like the length, number of illustrations, and expected completion date. A discursive table of contents, sample chapters (including your great introductory chapter and a substantive chapter from the heart of the book), and your curriculum vitae should be included.

Your book prospectus is a selling document. Use it to excite the editor. In social science, this means momentarily stepping out of the research culture and talking about your proposed book not as a specimen of scientific inquiry to be analyzed but as a book to provoke, to be debated, fought over, and studied. In choosing books, we editors are always looking for new ways of conveying knowledge about important topics. We seek books that contain new information and perspectives that our readers—social scientists, intellectuals, and students—need to know.

We would like to refer you to Great Proposals of the Past, but great proposals, unlike books themselves, never make it into the folklore of the scholarly publishing culture. Maybe this is so because these great proposals become good books and extinguish themselves in the process. The point is this: If your book is about labor movements in Western European industrial democracies after the war, you've got to use the few pages afforded to you in a proposal to demonstrate not only why this topic is worthy of readers' attention but why what you have to say about it will enrich their intellectual lives. If you are writing on theoretical debates within a field—say, cultural anthropology—you need to make a strong case for why one more book will really move the debate forward. In international relations, for example, there are countless manuscripts on the differences between realist, neorealist, liberal, and constructivist approaches to understanding world politics. Any editor must ask whether we need more books on these debates or whether the profession would do better to swear off these discussions for some period of time.

You've got to tell us a story about why the panel data or regression analyses or prisoner's dilemmas in this or that study matter. If you've never written a book proposal, it can't hurt to ask a senior social science colleague (not your advisor) whom you know to be a successful author to share one with you and perhaps to read and critique yours before you send it off to prospective editors. Trusted advisors—experienced senior social scientists who have traversed the learning curve of successful book publication—can also be valuable allies in helping you identify the right social science editor.

WHAT'S A SOCIAL SCIENCE EDITOR?

Social science editors like the authors of this chapter people the Accidental Profession, book publishing. As the old saying goes, nobody ever went to school to become a publisher. Social science editors typically find their jobs in one of two ways: they migrate out of academia into publishing, as one of us (Myers) did; or they come up through the ranks of publishing (as Dougherty, a former bartender and once young textbook salesman, did). We love our work and enjoy the great variety of intelligent and creative people with whom we do business every day. Veteran social science editors become quite knowledgeable about their fields. At Princeton University Press, we have four Ph.D.'s among our editors—(including Myers's new one from Michigan). Dougherty, an economics editor, recently threw caution and all good sense to the wind and published his own book about the relationship of the civic writings of Adam Smith to some of the new work now being done in economics.

As we build our lists, we develop and maintain ongoing relations and even good friendships among our networks of authors and advisors. In addition to our work in reading submissions, we editors manage a cumbersome review process and remain involved in the production and marketing of the books we sign. Some of us work in organizations that would test the mettle of the most zealous bureaucrat.

What do social science editors in scholarly presses look for in books? We look for pathbreaking scholarship or the important incremental additions to knowledge whose publication is significant to our editorial fields. We look for books that might cross disciplinary lines—although that is trickier than it sounds, for a successful cross-disciplinary book usually requires an author who is known across disciplines. We look for the book that is much anticipated, such as the next work of an economics Nobel laureate, or for the book a field needs, such as the next great urban sociology book. We look sometimes for the heterodox book. We look for books that fit the personality of our lists. This is an important but elusive criterion. Every editor's list is different. Social science is a fluid and flexible enterprise. So is its publishing. There are mostly Marxist geography lists, highly historical sociology lists, very technical economics lists, postmodernist anthropology lists, and so on. Identifying an editor by the personality of his or her list is a very important consideration for aspiring authors. What makes good sense in Ithaca or Toronto may land with a thud in Berkeley or Chapel Hill.

We urge you to become keen observers of the social science publishing scene. Learn about the culture of scholarly publishing in the *Chronicle of Higher Education* and other periodicals such as the *New York Review of Books*, the *Economist*, and the *Times Literary Supplement*. The bigger a fan you become of social science and social analysis in general, the more you'll learn about scholarly publishers because academic social science and its publishing culture are so inextricably and intimately joined. Since you are already a social scientist, you are probably steeped in the periodical literature of your home discipline, so learning about publishers is merely a matter of paying attention to mentions of publishers (ads, reviews, articles, stories, etc.) in periodicals and making the necessary connections. That can be fun.

We social science editors follow our disciplines (and contiguous social science disciplines) carefully. We read the journals, stay current with books from competing publishers, attend relevant talks on campus, and counsel regularly with experts in our fields. There's no free lunch for our lunch guests. We editors are always attuned to new information about exciting books, trends, and new authors for our lists. We attempt to identify the best prospects early. We also pay attention to what is being published elsewhere and how it is being received. We study what goes on in the publishing and academic cultures of other countries and around the world. We consult, though we do not conspire, with our competitors. We keep one eye on the public policy culture. We live in the real world and read widely for pleasure but also for a sense of what our discipline might contribute outside the academy.

BUSINESS 101

In acquiring books, social science editors try to balance scholarly and commercial considerations. There are some very good scholarly works that we cannot publish because we cannot sell enough copies to come close to recouping the press's costs. As library sales decline, we must increasingly rely on individual purchases and course adoptions to justify publication. These are larger but riskier markets. Internet sales outlets do not enlarge the market for scholarly social science books, although they do make it easier for people around the world to buy these specialized books. Price, too, is less of a predictor of sales success than basic economic theory might suggest. Price tolerances differ widely from field to field. Some books, especially in technical fields such as economics or psychology, tolerate relatively elastic prices. Then there is the paperback question. The folkloric notion in social science that paperbacks sell better than hardbacks is just that: folklore. Paperback publication is not the panacea to price resistance that it is often thought to be. We have published more titles in paperback than we would like to mention that sold less well than they did in cloth. To succeed in paper, most books must have steady, relatively large, and easily accessible course adoption markets (unless they are mysteries or romance novels).

We are, in the end, a business. Scholarly publishing is a consumer product industry, though we keep that quiet. We must keep our costs and revenue in line if we are to survive. To make matters more difficult, in our business, unlike most consumer product businesses, each product—each book—is unique in many ways, requiring separate and special attention in its acquisition, production, and marketing. We build our lists and specialize in certain areas on the principle that books related in subject matter will have similar results in the marketplace and will share market expenses—exhibits, meetings, mailings, ads—and thus enable us to achieve some economies of scale, however modest.

By choosing to publish the books we do, social science editors play an indirect role in the process of hiring, tenure, and promotion in the academy. Our criteria for picking books overlap to a great extent with the criteria for hiring and tenure. But they are by no means the same. We must sell a healthy number of books to survive. We must consider economic factors in our publishing decisions. Most universities are no longer inclined to subsidize presses, so university presses typically are compelled to find a mix of books that will cover the expenses. We appear to be at the cusp of a major change in the relationship between scholarly publishing and the tenure and review process. Some observers, including the president of the Modern Language Association, have questioned the primacy of the book for the tenure process, given the difficulties associated with getting a book published in many fields, though how this will play out remains to be seen. For the time being, books prevail.

University presses have limited capacity—each editor can work on only a certain number of books—and presses must maintain a balance among their various lists both for financial reasons and to meet the demand for publication across many disciplines. We cannot publish across all areas because we have only limited resources to produce and market books. Each new field we add requires additional marketing resources for activities such as exhibiting at meetings, advertising in journals, direct mail, and publicity. It does not make sense to engage in these activities for one or two titles. Thus there are going to be perfectly good projects that cannot be published by one press but that might be good candidates elsewhere.

The current pressure on social scientists to produce early books often does not permit a scholar to build a reputation with articles and talks and to season ideas, both of which make for a more successful book. Hence, the initial approach to the right editor is critical. The best way to approach a social science editor is through a common contact—that trusted senior social scientist colleague who has been there and who has the ear of the right editors at the appropriate publishers.

Neither of us merely picks and chooses among proposals that appear at our door. We go out and work with excellent scholars to develop book ideas on topics of current scholarly interest. We invite work by scholars of excellent reputation. We try to achieve a balance between junior and senior scholars, between subfields, and among scholarly, text, and general interest titles. A great scholarly list includes all these elements. We can publish only a limited number of revised dissertations. Due to their often narrow and highly technical coverage of topics, they simply do not sell as well as other kinds of scholarly work. But let us be clear: revised dissertations are fundamental to our mission. They are as much a part of the best scholarly social science lists as any other kind of book because they represent fresh and exciting ideas.

OTHER PATHS

University press editors are not the only possible contacts for publication of social science manuscripts. Another useful approach to editorial attention, especially in the social sciences, is through series editors. There is a proud and lively tradition of successful book series in social science, and many distinguished scholars, in their role as series editors, have helped nurture whole bodies of knowledge into being. One thinks, for example, of the sociologist Charles Tilly, whose venerable series Studies in Social Discontinuity, which included Immanual Wallerstein's classic work *The Modern World-System*, is a model for this sort of publishing. Another particularly notable series editor is Anthony Giddens, the distinguished British sociologist who now serves as director of the London School of Economics. Giddens was so successful in his early efforts as a series editor that eventually he joined forces with two of his social science colleagues, the political theorists John Thompson and David Held, and together they began their own publishing firm, Polity Press.

Yet another avenue to publication for a certain subset of social science authors is the public policy institute: organizations such as the Brookings Institution, the Urban Institute in Washington, D.C., RAND in Santa Monica, or the Social Market Foundation in London. These organizations sport specialized presses and employ editors attuned to the policy readership, which for some authors-to-be is, at least in part, the right audience. Such presses are not for everyone, but part of the lesson in studying the geography of scholarly social science publishing is that the landscape is complex and varied. For virtually every subfield there are excellent and distinguished series at presses of all shapes and sizes. Take an experienced, trusted senior colleague to lunch and draw as much useful information, both in terms of the publishing scene in general and in terms of individual book editors and academic series editors, as possible. You may even want to ask your colleague if you can use his or her name in approaching editors. Put some network theory into practice.

Still one more route to publication is through scholarly journals. Some social science fields are less book driven than others. For example, one of us, Dougherty, the Princeton economics editor, receives at most eight or nine unsolicited manuscript proposals a month and spends much more time approaching senior economists and commissioning their books. Books are not important to tenure and promotion in economics, but scholarly articles are. Myers, the Princeton political science editor, receives as many as five unsolicited proposals a day. Books make careers in political science, sociology, and most of the other social sciences. Since career building in economics (or in psychology) is different, so are the publishing requirements. Because of their theoretical and empirical foundations, these two fields resemble the natural sciences in their cultures more than they do their kindred social sciences. Articles in scholarly journals such as the *Journal of Political Economy* and the *Quarterly Journal of Economics* are the main stepping stones toward tenure and promotion in economics. Here we have neither the space nor, frankly, the direct experience in journals publishing to comment with authority on the proposal and placement of scholarly articles. Still, we mention a few things that aspiring economists should know.

The people who edit scholarly journals are not employees of university presses like us but senior scholars employed by university departments. The review process for journal articles is notably rigorous and notoriously time-consuming—so much so that a movement is afoot within economics to accelerate the approval and publication process through electronic publication. Scholarly journals vary greatly in subject matter and status. Identifying the appropriate journal for one's academic work requires careful consultation with advisors and senior colleagues. Finally, many successful book authors in economics build their books around closely related (and appropriately revised) published articles, working papers, and lecture notes. So while economists seldom think of book possibilities in their effort to place their articles, in the long run this work can figure into the publication of books.

THE PASSION THING

Fast-forward to your contract. You've found a good match with an editor at a good press, your book fits this editor's list, you've got a reasonable contract, and you're ready to place your manuscript in the ceremonial manila envelope and send it off for production. Then what happens? What should you expect of your editor and his or her fellow publishers in bringing your book to market?

Aside from the zillions of details attending the editing, design, production, marketing, publicizing, and selling of your book, your editor's passion for your book can make a real difference. By *passion* we mean that your editor understands what you are trying to accomplish intellectually with your book, gets excited about your intellectual goal, can explain to others what you are trying to accomplish with your book and how you go about it, knows the means of reaching the reviewers and readers whose attention you will need for accomplishing your intellectual goal, and will work the system and fight for your book. You need a champion as an editor, and if you have one you are likely to see your book well served.

PLUGGED NICKEL

Will a beautifully wrought new monograph on Durkheim's analysis of class or V. O. Key's methodology in studies of voting behavior, launched by a great first chapter, published in just the right series, and championed by a keen and zealous editor change the buying habits of social science book readers and thereby open up the market for our reluctant used book dealer mentioned above? Probably not. As any sophomore social science major knows, market activity is rarely explained by one factor, and the market for monographs is no different in this respect. However, if our scholarly social science monographs are not well conceived and written, well packaged and published, it is unlikely that anybody will want to read, much less buy them. A change in the commercial climate will have to wait. Until then, we will have to settle for the satisfaction inherent in getting the job done right.

8

FROM PARTICLES TO ARTICLES

THE INSIDE SCOOP ON SCIENTIFIC PUBLISHING

Trevor Lipscombe

The Clever Men of Oxford
Know all there is to be know'd
But they none of them know half as much
As intelligent Mr. Toad
              Kenneth Grahame,
      The Wind in the Willows, 1908

The oral examination is over and any necessary corrections have been carried out. With the appropriate forms signed, a graduate student is now transformed into a card-carrying Ph.D. She is not yet a scholar, but she is entering the last phase of the journey. What lies ahead is the rocky road to publication.

Scientists, as a rule, do not get tenure through writing books. They must rack up a suitable number of important articles in high-quality, peer-reviewed journals. While some universities, such as Harvard, ask a tenure-track professor to pick out her ten most influential articles, the majority still wish to see a long string of published, preferably impressive, papers. The rule of thumb for a research university is about three articles per year. Smaller colleges, perhaps more oriented toward teaching and involving undergraduates in professorial research activities, might settle for fewer articles, perhaps only one per year. Still, a person with a freshly minted Ph.D. will probably have to spend a few years doing hard labor on the temporary postdoc circuit before obtaining a tenure-track position; merely to go from one short, fixed-term appointment to another requires an ongoing record of publications. How can a young scholar rise to such a challenge?

The first step is to assess accurately how many articles may come from the Ph.D. thesis work. Clearly, any paper of seminal importance would, or should, have been whisked off to a major journal such as *Nature* or *Science* by the Ph.D. advisor, with the student as a coauthor. For a physicist, a research result of profound importance may not have been sent to *Nature*, which proclaims to publish articles of interest to all scientists, but may instead have been dispatched to a letters journal, such as *Physical Review Letters* (*PRL*) or, in Europe, to *Physics Letters* (*Phys. Letts.*). Each division of science has its own equivalent of *PRL* or *Phys. Letts.*—a vehicle for the swift publication of pathbreaking research results. Medical research, for example, has the *New England Journal of Medicine* or, in Europe, the *Lancet*.

It may be tempting to regard the publication of thesis findings in a rapid-communication journal as somewhat of a triumph, but the work should not stop there. An article in *Nature* or *Physical Review Letters* is perforce brief. It provides only a sketch of an important result. In many cases, the key point or the cornerstone of such a paper is a diagram showing the theoretical explanation of a previously observed phenomenon; an experimental verification of previously abstract theory; or a description of some novel behavior that no one has heretofore recorded. The author should regard the result deemed worthy of publication by *Nature* as only the first step. There is a need for a fuller explanation or explication of the research, showing all the theoretical underpinnings or the details of the experimental setup and results, or the computational techniques employed. Assuming this brings to light some extra science, rather than being a vacuous rehash of the rapid publication, this new article would warrant publication in an archival research journal. In the case of physics, the *Journal of Physics* or *Physical Review* would be the place to go. Even then, there may still be more publishable material. If, after publication of the archival article takes place, an afterthought occurs, this may form another article. Essentially an addendum to the two previous articles, it may not warrant a full paper in its own right; some journals, though, have a "research notes" or "brief reports" section to accommodate such papers. In many ways, papers published in these sections mark the end of a line of research, just as a letters or rapid-communications section marks the beginning.

Let me use my own experience to illustrate. I was once invited to apply a piece of statistics known as "run theory" to a set of experiments on nuclear decay. Run theory, while a basic mathematical tool of statistical control theory used in industrial engineering, is virtually unknown in physics. (It serves as a standard statistical test for the fairness of slot machines in Las Vegas!) While we all know that a fair coin, if tossed one hundred times, will come down roughly fifty times heads and fifty times tails, run theory allows you to predict how many runs of straight heads there will be, and of what length these runs are, for any chain of *N* tosses. As a theoretical physicist by training, I know that any time you bring in some unusual piece of mathematics into physics, you usually have a publishable paper. By applying run theory to quantum decay, we were able to test in a new way the randomness, or lack thereof, in nuclear decay. The result was published in a letters journal, *Physics Letters A.*

Part of the challenge, though, was to modify the previously existing run theory, mostly developed in the 1940s, to suit our needs. Also, the experiments were far from simple to carry out. Added to that, while one could merely make reference to run theory in a letters article, some physicists reading the article would not seek out those references. The remedy: a far more complete paper, showing the experimental details and results in full, with a complete working out of run theory. This was published in *Physical Review A.*

There was, though, another venue for publication. While most high school mathematics and physics teachers know that a fair coin has a 50 percent chance of coming down heads, are they aware of the predictions of run theory? Probably not. In a wonderful pedagogical moment, you can ask the students in a class, as homework, to toss a coin twenty times and record the sequence of heads and tails. Run theory is a spectacular, almost foolproof, way to determine which students actually did the experiment and which faked the results. With such an intriguing lead-in, a paper on run theory aimed at physics teachers in high schools or community colleges seemed appropriate, and thus we published a fun paper in the *Physics Teacher,* in which the mathematics was stripped down to the bare essentials.

One type of article was notable by its absence. It would have been possible, I think, to have written a long review article on the applications of run theory to modern physics. To do so would have required a few weeks in the library, searching out the foundational articles in run theory (published in a mix of statistics and engineering journals) and tracking down some of the more successful applications of run theory in the physical sciences, broadly conceived. Then one could have composed a mature, definitive article that elucidated the origins and mathematical underpinnings of run theory, detailed its applications in a variety of fields, and referred to the two published articles in *Physics Letters A* and *Physical Review A* before sketching possible other applications to systems currently of interest to physicists. Such a review article would have been appropriate for *Physics Reports*, *Reviews of Modern Physics*, or *Reports on the Progress of Physics*.

Most doctoral theses contain similar possibilities. The central spark of the thesis might well warrant rapid publication. Virtually all of the chapters could appear in an archival journal. (If not, a Ph.D. should not have been granted!) Some chapters might contain theory or experiments that could be intriguing to a nonresearch community (for which pedagogical journals would be appropriate), and any further research on the same topic could be handled by a research note or brief report. The introduction of the thesis, where a student typically "shows what she knows," possesses all the hallmarks of a review article: the student shows in the introduction that she has surveyed the literature and that she knows what the main important topic is, what minor topic her thesis addresses, and what large, unsolved problems remain. And the step from a published review article to the publication of a book, an item that will grace the résumé of any scholar throughout the remainder of her academic life, is but a short one. What's

more, while humanities and social science publishers may spurn
the work of young scholars (for a variety of reasons), it is unusual
for a good science book not to be published.

Last, an experimentalist has probably spent six years coaxing
and cajoling some beast of a machine to generate meaningful results. Often, the experimental device has to be adjusted, manipu-
lated, or enticed to rise phoenixlike from the ashes of some other
device in order to do the job. This process might merit description in an article for a device-oriented journal, such as *Reviews of
Scientific Instruments* or the *Journal of Applied Physics.* Likewise, a
theoretician often has to transcend pencil and paper these days,
solving the equations she generates not only in her head but also
by computer. Computers can sometimes verge on the ornery, and
getting them to crunch the numbers for certain types of equations
can be a formidable challenge. It may be that, to get the solutions
she needed, a young researcher has overcome a computational
problem encountered, or soon to be encountered, by many others. Consequently, an article in a journal like *Computers in Physics*
might be called for.

While I would like to encourage creativity in publishing—
recognition that a single piece of research might generate a relatively large number of papers—I do not advocate publishing
work piecemeal. Dashing off a "thought of the day" for publication might have worked as a strategy for getting tenure in the
past, but it seems not to be the wave of the future. When a friend
recently described a fellow faculty member by saying, "He never
has an unpublished thought," it was not meant as a compliment.
If other universities follow Harvard's lead and request copies of
the most influential papers, it behooves a young scholar not to
publish important results in dribs and drabs. A smaller number of

seminal contributions rather than a larger number of average ones is what's called for. My own doctoral thesis, which sits accumulating dust in the Radcliffe Science Library at Oxford, was a shameful case in point. In retrospect, my main work was the application of a recondite piece of mathematics to three interesting (to me) turbulent physical systems. The net result was to publish three papers, each of which was of the "math + application" species. By the time I began to write up the last paper, I had lost interest. A far better use of my time would have been to publish one letters paper, which simply announced that by applying a certain mathematical technique, one could obtain a set of intriguing results in turbulence theory. A second paper would explicate the mathematics, with three brief applications to turbulence at the end. A final publication could have been a review article called "New Developments in Turbulence," which would discuss various inroads made by topologists into turbulence, citing some of my own results, but mainly those that inspired my original research. A tenure committee staring at the papers that I *did* publish might easily have mistaken them for photocopies of each other, which would not have boded well. The scheme outlined above—a letter, an archival article, and a review article—is distinctly different and, I feel, might influence a tenure committee more favorably.

WHERE SHOULD YOU SUBMIT?

Songwriter Sammy Cahn, who wrote such classics as "High Hopes," was once asked which came first, the lyrics or the melody. His response was "the check." This is useful advice. Rather than write an article and then determine whether it should go to a rapid-communication journal or an archival journal, and which one, it is much better to decide on the journal first. Your colleagues should help. If you sum up your main research result to them and the response is lethargy or ennui, then perhaps you need to write an archival paper. If the folks in your field within your department prick up their ears, then perhaps a letters journal within your own discipline is the right venue. But if your seminar on a new high-temperature superconductor, for instance, draws researchers from the physics, chemistry, and materials science departments, and they acclaim your work with great praise, then perhaps it's time to dash off a missive to *Nature*.

It is important to clarify the importance of your research *before* you write it up for publication. *Nature* will need to have a cover letter and an abstract that makes it abundantly clear what you have done, why you have done it, and why the result is of prime importance to a broad range of scientists. The in-house editors at *Nature* have science degrees and will probably look carefully at the paper before sending it out to referees. A majority of papers sent to *Nature* or *Science* fail to make it out for peer review. While many researchers may like to think of it as poor taste or incompetence on the part of the in-house editorial staff, it probably isn't. The staff are swamped with far more articles than they can hope to publish, and poorly written, poorly explained ones are dead on arrival. After all, why would they want to suck up the valuable time of a referee, and use up some of the journal's goodwill, sending an article out for review whose chance of publication they consider slim to none? So if you find yourself rejected by *Nature* but are convinced that your research is of the utmost interest and importance, it may be time to swallow your pride and take a stab at rewriting the material. As the great Russian (astro)physicist Ya. B. Zel'dovich is alleged to have said, "If you can't explain your work to a bright high school student, then you don't understand it." To paraphrase him for publishing purposes, "If you can't explain your work to a bright science graduate, then you can forget the premier science journals."

After you've chosen a rapid-communication journal, another main point is length. Broad-circulation magazines raise money not only by sales but also by advertising. The two go hand in hand, for the larger the number of copies sold, the more the magazine can charge advertisers. In the challenging financial world of corporate publishing today, it may be tough to get a long, or long-winded, article published. At this stage, bear in mind the cliché that a picture is worth a thousand words. Your main result might be forcefully expressed in terms of only a few diagrams. The mathematics might be collapsed down to the starting and concluding equations. Computational niceties can be omitted. This strategy helps to highlight your result more forcibly, succinctly, and with a minimum of technical material or jargon. Such measures enhance your chance of publication in a science magazine but also ensure that there will be plenty of unpublished material on reserve for your next paper in the archival journal.

Whether you have chosen a rapid-publication journal, archival journal, research note, review article, or book as the appropriate way to convey your research, the writing remains. It is important to identify the specific journal to which you plan to submit the finished article, as this can have ramifications for the peer-review process. For example, if most of the research work you have built on was published in the *Journal of Experimental Psychology*, it presumably makes sense to submit your own work to that journal.

When I worked for a physics journal, I was baffled by the number of submissions we received that contained no articles from our journal in the list of references. If, instead, a submission had many references to a sister (rival) journal, I suspected that the sister journal had already rejected the paper. Also, as the journal I worked for was rather prestigious, it seemed odd that no, or only a few, references were made to other work that we had published. The two concerns, combined, made me question the scholarship of the new submission, which would provoke me to select a tougher reviewer from our pool of manuscript readers.

There are other aspects of journal selection. Even among archival journals, where completeness and correctness are the requirements for publication (rather than importance or broad appeal), some journals will elicit more kudos and look far better on your résumé than others. Some journals rank far higher in terms of the average number of citations to the articles they publish. As many tenure committees are increasingly concerned about the number of citations to your articles and the so-called impact factor of the journals in which you publish, it might be advisable to look at such matters ahead of time. For those with tenure, it sometimes is more rewarding to publish in a journal that is actually read than in one that is often cited. One can publish articles on liquid crystals, for example, in *Physical Review A* or the journal *Liquid Crystals*. Each issue of the former has roughly the same dimensions as a telephone directory; the latter, in comparison, is a mere pamphlet. *Liquid Crystals* is far more likely to be read in its entirety by researchers in the field than *Physical Review A*. This may not be a problem if your article is squarely in the liquid-crystals section of *Phys. Rev.*, but if your work on their optical properties appears in the optics section instead, your work may be overlooked by precisely the audience you had most hoped it would reach.

This raises another issue, related to interdisciplinary articles. While many archival journals devote a section to papers of general interest, these are often neglected by scholars who turn to the subsection of the journal that reports work of interest in their specific field. One could submit, instead, to an interdisciplinary journal, such as the *Proceedings of the Royal Society A*, which caters to physicists, chemists, mathematicians, and engineers. The *Proceedings of the National Academy of Sciences* is similar. Fortunately, such problems are obviated by the widespread access of online journals. To find an article of interest, one need only perform a search across all the journals your library has access to. At the very least, the titles, authors, and abstracts will appear. There are also electronic alerting services, available from either publishers or electronic aggregators, that notify a researcher of all papers published in a particular field. In principle, therefore, a researcher should be able to locate your new paper no matter where it is published.

Having selected a journal, please read some of the articles it contains, front to back. It is important to know how to write for the journal you have chosen. The story is told of Sir Horace Lamb, Victorian doyen of fluid mechanics, that upon the publication of his definitive tome *Hydrodynamics*, which ran to several hundred pages, one Cambridge wag remarked that you could read the book in its entirety and never realize that water was wet. Lamb's tradition is carried on in the *Journal of Fluid Mechanics*. *JFM*, as it is known, has a tendency to view liquids and gases as beautiful mathematical structures rather than physical entities. Thus, should you wish to send them a paper, it is important to use the formal mathematics that they like. An article that looks at how a surfactant is absorbed onto the surface of a liquid droplet, if expressed in terms of tensor analysis and the properties of Geigenbauer polynomials and creatures of that ilk, may appeal to the editors and readers of *JFM*. If, instead, one is concerned with the molecular interactions between the droplets and the surface, perhaps the *Journal of Colloid and Interface Science* will be more appropriate. I once had a paper rejected from a pedagogical physics journal (these are, I believe, more difficult to publish in than research journals). The referee reported that the system I analyzed was historically and philosophically important and that the result was "neat" and correct. The stumbling block? The level of mathematics needed was far above that of the articles published in the journal. As I couldn't obtain the same result using a simpler set of mathematical tools, my article was dead in the water. Realistically, I should have recognized, once I had obtained my result, that it was not appropriate for a research journal and too advanced mathematically for a pedagogical journal. If I had thought more fully beforehand, I would have realized it was not worth my time to write the work up for publication.

SUBMISSION AND REVIEW

After the research is completed, the journal selected, and the paper written, what next? A variety of submission procedures are in place, and the Web page of the journal, or often the January issue of the print edition, will contain instructions on the actual procedure. This is important material to read, especially for a neophyte author. If you wish to see your work in print rapidly, it certainly helps to follow the instructions of a letters-type journal "to the letter."

For a rapid-publication journal, you should expect the in-house editorial staff to become involved, as mentioned above. If they are not convinced of broad appeal or importance, the paper may go no further. If, on the other hand, they are persuaded that your paper has merit, it may be sent out to two readers. In a cover letter, you may have suggested the names of people to whom your paper could, or indeed shouldn't, be sent. Rest assured, the editorial staff are under no obligation to honor any of your requests. With the reports in, the journal staff will contact you again. If the readings are negative, you will receive a rejection letter. While most journals have an appeals process, and you could vigorously defend yourself to the editorial oversight committee, it's not usually worth your effort. A simpler approach is to shake the dust from your feet and submit the article somewhere else. If it is accepted, you can bask in the knowledge that you were right. If you get a second set of negative readings, perhaps your work isn't quite so wonderful as you had thought, and it's time for you to head back to the lab.

If both reports are favorable, you may have to tweak your article a bit, but then you will be published, with international fame and glory awaiting you. Typically, though, given the slings and arrows of the peer-review process, there will be one favorable and one negative report. I once received three readings on a manuscript of mine. One opined "publish as is," another recommended "do not publish," and the third, sitting firmly on the fence, deemed the manuscript "publishable with minor revisions." In short, I garnered a yes, a no, and a maybe. With such a mixed bag of reviews, the letter from the journal staff will possibly indicate what direction they are leaning toward. Usually, though, you will be expected to revise and resubmit the paper, pointing out what you have changed and why, and what you declined to change and why.

For some reason, it's traditional for journals to send the revised manuscript and the author's response back to the reader who balked at publication of the original manuscript. There are therefore a couple of do's and don'ts to remember. First, always be polite. I never cease to be amazed by the vitriolic author responses to seemingly innocuous readers' reports. Such letters often berate the editorial staff ("You chose an incompetent, biased referee who has no idea of the importance of my research. You should have sent it to Professor Dubyoski instead, as I told you." Nine times out of ten, it's Professor Dubyoski who read the manuscript and hated it.) Another frequent response is, "I know who you chose for a reader. It's Professor Zanella, evil incarnate, who has vindictively assassinated my papers since I spilt coffee on him at a conference twenty years ago." Ten times out of ten, Professor Zanella was the referee who wrote the glowingly positive report in favor of publication.

Of course, people who write inappropriate responses to referees' comments are sometimes chosen as referees themselves. If you receive a report that suggests publication will be appropriate if you read and cite five pathbreaking papers, all written by Professor Davis, then Professor Davis may well be the journal's reviewer. It would be politic, therefore, to add the citations. It is sometimes, however, appropriate to use the academic equivalent of "It's my toy, so I get to play with it." In the end, *you* are the author of the article, not the referee. If you prefer to use, say, a differential equation and the referee prefers you to use its Fourier transform, then you may want to assert your right to the differential equation. If both lead to the same result, with the same economy, and with the same intellectual appeal, then why switch? Stating your preference clearly, without being high- or heavy-handed, should convince the reader, the journal staff, or both.

With most articles, it's usually a two-step process. With an initial positive report and the corrections made, normally only one further round of revisions is necessary before acceptance. Then it's simply a case of handing over the manuscript and/or electronic files and waiting for the copyediting, typesetting, and production processes to begin.

Finally . . . there's an old adage that it's not what you know, it's who you know. When your paper is published, you may receive some offprints. In the modern era, you should have electronic files. It is a good idea to ship these to any person whose work you have cited. After all, if your paper builds on their work, and you have been found worthy of publication, the other researchers should presumably be interested in your work. In principle, they probably will come across your work anyway, but perhaps not. Why take the chance? Introduce yourself at a conference, or via mail or e-mail, and send them your latest published pieces. It should increase the chance of your work being cited, which is good in and of itself, but it will also forge links between you and other groups of researchers. Together you may come up with a new line of publishable research that you can pursue together. At the very least, it may enhance your chance of finding another postdoc position or perhaps a tenure-track slot.

One last request. Science journals, as any librarian will tell you, are almost prohibitively expensive. Even moderately sized university libraries are facing budget cuts and having to cancel subscriptions to major journals. Libraries in developing countries cannot possibly hope to afford such luxuries. It is true that some North American and European libraries sometimes donate old copies of print journals to libraries in developing nations, but "old" can mean five years out of date. So if you know of any research groups at African or Asian universities, please send them a copy of your recent paper, whether you cite their research or not. My friends in Bhutan and Zimbabwe assure me that their major challenge is not getting published in reputable journals but keeping apace of what research is being done currently in North American and European universities. In sending copies of your work to scholars in the developing world, you will fulfill what Daniel Coit Gilman, founder of the Johns Hopkins University Press, proclaimed to be the university's "noble duty": to disseminate knowledge, not only to "those who can attend the lectures, but far and wide."

Some great scientists have eschewed publication. Fitzgerald, of the Lorentz-Fitzgerald contraction made famous in Einstein's special theory of relativity, would present his work orally to the Royal Society in London but seldom stooped to publication. Rather like Saint Simeon Stylites, who spent many years atop a sixty-foot-tall column prostrating himself during his waking hours, Mr. Fitzgerald is to be admired rather than emulated. Put another way, Mr. Toad may indeed know more than the intelligent men and women of Oxford, but unless he has a decent publication record, he still won't get tenure!

9

ILLUSTRATED IDEAS

PUBLISHING IN THE ARTS

Judy Metro

As good a place as any to begin a discussion about publishing dissertations in the visual arts is at the source: the submissions pile on the desk of a university press art editor. The first thing we notice, with relief, is that the pile is not about to topple. This is because it does not contain actual completed manuscripts. Those are on the floor (you see where I'm going) or on the couch if the editor is lucky enough to have one. The submissions pile is where every working day the art editor learns just enough about a book project to assign it to heaven (pursue it!), purgatory (ponder), or hell (purge it). The author of a first book has to be knocking on the right door with a very compelling book proposal to get into heaven, because here's what else might be in the submissions pile at any given time: two other compelling proposals for first books; five proposals invited by the editor from seasoned scholars; proposals solicited by the editor for three or four museum exhibition catalogues; two proposals for trade titles inspired by the publisher's recent lists, one of them solicited, the other a pleasant surprise; one proposal for a regional or campus-related book; and a few obvious candidates for the purge pile.

As others in this volume have noted, the acquisitions editor is not awaiting submissions but rather seeking them out, inviting them, competing mightily for the best of them. It follows that the editor's interest is already attached to many of the items in the submissions pile and that further pursuit of at least these projects is nearly certain. In this situation, how does the idea for a first book, specifically for a revised dissertation, capture and maintain the interest of the art editor?

First, let's go back to the editor's office. No matter how excellent a revised dissertation might be, its unannounced arrival (complete with a set of 160 photocopied illustrations) is a thud on the editor's floor, and not the best first handshake. Just as the author considered which publishers to approach, so the editor wants a chance to consider which manuscripts to solicit for a full reading and evaluation. An additional reason not to send an unsolicited visual arts manuscript to the publisher is that they tend to be voluminous once combined with their picture programs, expensive and impractical to give and receive without an invitation.

The place to start, then, is the book proposal, the critical document for getting a foot in the door at a university press. What makes a strong book proposal in the arts? Certainly all the criteria outlined by the contributors to this volume pertain to a proposal in the arts: a good fit with the publisher's list, a concise and engaging summary, a clear rationale for the author's approach, a roundup of current literature on the topic and a sound reason to add said book to it, an impressive curriculum vitae, a realistic assessment of the audiences and markets for the book, a projected manuscript length of well under 350 double-spaced pages including notes, and a reasonable time frame for delivery. Attached to the proposal, which by the time it is read should have inspired the editor to want to learn more, are the introductory chapter and perhaps one from the interior of the study, a sampling of the kinds of illustrations planned for the book (photocopies will do), and a narrative outline of the entire work. Before turning to additional areas that need to be addressed in the visual arts proposal, we should examine what exactly is special about books on the arts, from the perspective of both the publisher and the author.

What sets apart books in the visual arts from other scholarly books is of course their visual component. While authors of books on art theory, aesthetics, and methodology may do without illustrations altogether, they are the exceptions in this field. Authors of most books on the fine arts (painting, drawing, printmaking, photography, sculpture, and the decorative arts), architecture, archeology, landscape architecture, design, and graphic arts will normally require illustrations both to deliver an overarching argument to the reader and to render specific points and comparisons. The same holds true for authors of books on the performing arts. In gift and coffee-table books, the images may have an alluring or decorative function, but in a revised dissertation, the images and the author's reading of them form as much a part of the *documentation* for the study as do the notes and bibliography.

Yet for any university press publisher, this visual component adds a thick layer of risk to the publishing enterprise because, as we all know, illustrations (especially in color) are costly to obtain, reproduce with permission, and print. What is less recognized is that illustrated books also compound the work of the acquisitions editor, manuscript editor, designer, production controller, and permissions coordinator; even the publicist, sales director, advertising manager, and fulfillment department feel the extra weight of an illustrated book in their budgets and on their schedules.[1] From the moment an illustrated book enters the publishing house as a manuscript to the time it leaves the publisher's warehouse destined for a customer (and sometimes boomerangs as a return), you can be sure that it will require more of everything a publishing house has to offer than will most nonillustrated titles. This is why many so university presses choose not to build lists in art or even to dabble in it.

The same holds true for the authors of books with illustrations. The process will draw from them a larger investment of time, money, know-how, and patience than will a nonillustrated project. An author once complained that it had taken her easily as long to count her illustrations, assign them a place and weight in the book, and label them as it had to write the hardest part of her book, namely the introduction. That of course was a sneeze compared to the time she spent on the most dreaded of all image-related chores: gathering photographs and reproduction rights for each illustration and handling the follow-up paperwork in several languages—not to mention paying for it all in several currencies.

Now it is true that while authors and publishers together carry a heavier assignment of risk in preparing and producing illus-

---

1. For example, promotion and sales budgets are tapped liberally for color proofs of sample illustrations and jackets, which review media, book clubs, magazines interested in serial rights, and buyers for chains and small accounts alike insist on seeing before making decisions or placing orders. Illustrated books, being generally of larger format, cost more to pack and transport, take up more space in the warehouse, and need to be kept in pristine condition to command their full price.

trated books, they also stand to reap higher benefits in due time *if* the books sell as expected. Of all books published by university presses, illustrated books may exert the strongest pull on a non-scholarly audience. They are more visible, agreeable, and attractive to the general reading audience than are many other kinds of scholarly books; as a result there is a slightly larger built-in audience for them. In addition, large-format illustrated books command a higher retail price and therefore bring in more revenue per copy sold than smaller format nonillustrated works. Given that royalties are computed on the net retail price of the book, the author receiving a standard 5 percent royalty on an art monograph stands to earn in dollar terms twice as much as the author of, say, a history monograph earning the same royalty rate. Considering the out-of-pocket expenses the first-time author of a visual arts study will encounter on the way to publication, this is just as it should be.

In this climate of intensified risk, it stands to reason that editors and their presses exercise special caution in selecting illustrated titles for their list. To be sure, an art editor will be more impressed with an excellent book proposal if it also shows its author to have prepared for the realities of planning and publishing an illustrated book. To get there, the author might begin by considering—and then addressing in the proposal—the following topics, each of which I will discuss in more detail below:

- Number and kind of illustrations (color, black and white, line drawings)
- Dispersal of illustrations within the book (scattered throughout, confined to a separate plate section, grouped on inserts)

- Estimated cost of photography and permissions
- Special problems (restrictions with photo permitters, living artists, or estates)
- Special events (related exhibitions, artist's anniversaries, other important forthcoming titles on the same subject)
- Sources of publication funding

The exploration of each of these topics is a must for anyone planning to submit a book proposal in the arts, as it will yield information that has a direct bearing on (1) the editing, design, production, and marketing of the book and (2) the book's budget and yours. It makes sense, then, to investigate each one in detail and to discuss how different decisions or outcomes reverberate through the publishing process.

Before we delve into these topics, it might be useful to outline briefly the division of responsibility between the author and the publisher with regard to illustrations. There are no hard-and-fast rules, but this is the situation you are likely to encounter with a revised dissertation:

AUTHOR'S RESPONSIBILITIES. The author is responsible for collecting, paying for, and providing the publisher with high-quality "camera copy" (a glossy black-and-white photograph, line drawing, 35 mm slide, or color transparency) for each illustration or with a digital file prepared to the publisher's technical specifications.[2] Glossies and slides are generally purchased outright from the

2. Camera copy, true to its name, was at one time placed in front of the printer's camera to produce the film from which printing plates are made. Today, the camera has been replaced with a scanner, and digital files have been added to the list of acceptable "camera copy" for some publishers. Nonetheless, it is still

source, but color transparencies are usually rented for periods of three to six months. The author of a first book should also be prepared to secure and pay for reproduction rights from the copyright holder of each illustration that is not in the public domain. (The fees vary widely and are significantly higher for color than for black-and-white reproductions. On average, the fee for camera copy and reproduction rights for a black-and-white glossy would range from $25 to $50 each; the same for a color transparency would range from $100 to $150 each, plus overdue rental fees of $25 per month.) The author is also responsible for paying artist's rights fees for twentieth-century artists who are living or who died less than seventy years before the projected publication date. (These fees also vary and are usually subject to negotiation with the artist's rights agency.) It is up to the author to determine what is in copyright and who needs to be paid, but the publisher can offer advice in that area and usually has a sample permissions request form with the information a copyright holder will want to know, such as expected print run and price of the book, target publication date, and what rights are being requested (e.g., English-language world rights, English-language rights in North America or the United Kingdom, world rights in all languages). The author is also responsible for returning camera copy to owners at the end of the publication process.

PUBLISHER'S RESPONSIBILITIES. The ultimate decision on the number and kind of illustrations and the method of printing them belongs

---

perfectly appropriate (and even preferred) that you submit flat, two-dimensional camera copy to your publisher.

to the publisher. The final decision on the jacket is the publisher's as well. The publisher is also responsible for paying for all printing costs associated with illustrations and for finding a subsidy, in consultation with the author, to support the publisher's plans with regard to illustrations. If, for example, the author desires a sixteen-page color insert and the publisher does not see it as a necessity, it will be up to the author to secure full funding for the color insert. If the publisher does support its inclusion, the publisher may join forces with the author to find a subsidy. The publishing contract may then include a clause that a color insert is contingent upon the author's (and/or publisher's) securing an outside subsidy for a certain amount. (By the same token, if the publisher's plans for the book's illustration program are more ambitious than the author's, it will be the publisher's responsibility to secure and pay for the additional camera copy and permissions as well as, of course, the printing.) The publisher is responsible for the camera copy while it is in its hands or the printer's.

NUMBER AND KIND OF ILLUSTRATIONS

How Many?

Whether you have written a book on Olmec art, Andrea del Verrocchio, New Delhi architecture, Eugène Atget, the Guerrilla Girls, or the music of Irving Berlin, you will need to think about the minimum number and kind of illustrations your argument requires. Working back from an ideal book length of 224 to 256 printed pages for a revised dissertation in the arts, the maximum number of illustrations should range from seventy-five to one hundred, figured roughly as follows: the average double-spaced typescript page contains 250 words and the average art-format (8 × 10 inch) printed page contains 500 words (700 or more for notes); a 350-page manuscript will thus yield from 160 to 175 book pages of text. If one-third of the illustrations are reproduced as full pages and two-thirds as half pages, we have added approximately 50 to 66 book pages to the count, bringing it from a low of 210 to a high of 240 pages. Allowing 14 or 16 pages for the front matter and an index brings us into the desired range of 224 to 256 book pages. (Most cases are not that tidy, but this is not far off.)

Try not to look at the maximum illustration count as a goal; it is perfectly acceptable and sometimes necessary to use fewer than seventy-five illustrations in your study. The important question to ask is how many (more pertinent, how few) illustrations are necessary to demonstrate and adequately support your thesis. The illustrations in a revised dissertation are not for display but for examination, and each one should reward the close reader of the text with a nugget of information. In other words, think of illustrations as you have been urged to think about footnotes. Use them judiciously and not to display everything that you have uncovered along the way, make them apt and compelling, and be sure they do support your conclusions. Remember that excessive illustration has the same effect as verbosity: it wearies the reader and tends to diffuse rather than to bring home a point.

Here too it is important to recognize the difference between your book audience and your dissertation committee. The latter may have required an exhaustive roundup of images in support of ideas, as well as an accounting of the steps that brought you to a certain conclusion. But your book audience does not expect the entire image bank and the roadmap. They expect the deft delivery of ideas with adequate support and documentation in the way of clear, well-chosen illustrations, just enough for them to see your point and judge the validity of your argument. In addition, the dissertation committee members are bound by their profession as well as their commitment to teaching to read your dissertation. The hoped-for book audience is much larger and, with the exception of family members, comes to the book voluntarily, expecting to be engaged and edified not only by your conveyance of ideas but by your ability to marshal images in support of those ideas.

Another criterion for including certain illustrations is their familiarity to your intended audience. The landmarks in Tibetan art will need to be illustrated, especially if your study reaches out to new audiences, whereas the iconic images of Western art may not require illustration.

Black-and-White or Color?

In asking what kinds of reproductions are appropriate in any one book, the issue of black-and-white versus color is usually paramount in the minds of the author and the publisher. Surely the first question to consider is what kinds of reproductions are appropriate for the subject matter of the book. Common sense dictates that a dissertation on the rise of eighteenth-century color printmaking requires some component of color to render its subject intelligible to the reader. On the other hand, black-and-white illustrations might be adequate for subjects that are plausibly rendered in a monochromatic scale, such as some architecture, sculpture, or photography. But for the wide range of books between these clear-cut examples, the choice of color versus black-and-white will almost always hinge on budgetary considerations.

In the best of worlds, four-color reproductions would grace every publication on art, if only for their documentary value. In reality, only those books with a sufficiently large museum or bookstore audience, or those with outside funding, will have budgets that allow for this. Although color finds its way into most illustrated books published today, economics may rule it out as a possibility for a revised dissertation except, perhaps, on the book's jacket or as a separate color insert. Because black-and-white illustrations—reproduced either as line cuts (blacks and whites with no shading, as in woodcuts and musical notations) or as halftones (with gradations of shading, as in paintings, washes, and photographs)—cost only slightly more to print than a page of text, they will most certainly carry the day. This does not mean, however, that they do not require more in terms of editing, design, and production attention than does a page of text, or that the glossies themselves and the reproduction rights will not cost the author a bundle to secure, or that the number of black-and-whites will be of little concern to the publisher.

Most studies on the fine arts cry out for at least three or four works to be reproduced in color, if for no other reason than as a guide to reading the "color" of the other works by the same artist or group that are reproduced in black and white elsewhere in the book. Understandably, many authors think they are being very reasonable when they cite the need for "only a few" color plates. It turns out, however, that three or four is not a rational number when it comes to color printing.[3] In addition, their inclusion will

3. Most first books are printed on a one- or two-color press on an uncoated or matte-coated sheet. Switching to a four-color press and a more expensive coated sheet for color more than doubles the cost regardless of how many color

drive up the unit cost, and therefore the retail price, without increasing the book's potential to sell more copies (i.e., including three color plates in a 256-page book will not add to its perceived value). It is better in this case to reserve color for the jacket, arguing for a color image on both the front and the back.

For an author whose book has a strong enough market to warrant color or an outside subsidy to underwrite the expense, a color insert might be an option. In this scenario, an eight- or sixteen-page section is printed separately on a four-color press and bound into the otherwise one-color book as a separate signature. An eight-page insert may include up to ten or twelve images, a sixteen-page insert twice as many, depending on how many images can be comfortably and legibly paired on a page.

Occasionally an editor will see a market for a book that would be well served by even more color illustrations than the author has dared to include in the count. A case in point would be an engagingly written dissertation that, with the addition of thirty or more color plates, has a chance to win a general readership in addition to an academic one. In this rare case, the decision might be made to include several color inserts or to print the entire book on a four-color press and scatter the color throughout. As the idea originated with the publisher, it would, as we noted above, be the publisher's responsibility to gather and pay for the additional color images required for this scheme.

---

images are included and is only worthwhile when a substantial number of color plates are scattered throughout the book. There are ways of printing just a portion of the book on a four-color press, and these will be mentioned below. Color tip-ins, printed separately from the rest of the book and then glued to a page at its inner margin, are also very costly, largely because of the handwork required to insert them into the book.

DISPERSAL OF ILLUSTRATIONS WITHIN THE BOOK
Black-and-White

Especially from the vantage point of the reader, the most satis-
factory and convenient method of positioning illustrations within
a book is to integrate them throughout so that the images are ad-
jacent to the text that refers to them. This is the prevalent method
for integrating black-and-white illustrations in art books, and it
is safe to assume this organization unless some other plan, such as
the one that follows, makes more sense for your book.

You will have noticed in your research that the illustrations in
older books are most often confined to a separate section labeled
"Plates." This was necessitated by printing methods that did not
easily marry text and images, but a separate illustration section or
sections may have merit even today for certain types of studies.
Grouped illustrations lend themselves readily to didactic purposes and comparative study. They are especially useful for a body
of works that are important to see side by side and in number but
about which the author has commentary that bears on the group
as a whole rather than on individual works. For example, in a dissertation comparing manifestations of the dada movement in
Berlin and Zurich, it might be advantageous to include separate
plate sections showing the work from each city rather than to
pose an elaborate series of comparisons throughout the book.

Grouping also presents an opportunity to economize on paper,
in that the text section (the bulk of the book) can be printed on a
less expensive uncoated stock. Relegating the photographs for a
dissertation on Henry Fox Talbot, for example, to a separate section printed on a fine stock might be a more elegant and eco-

ˈnomical alternative to printing the entire book on a mediocre stock.

Color

If color illustrations are in the picture, they will probably be confined to separate inserts, as we discussed above. Nevertheless, I outline the possibilities here, from most to least expensive.

The costliest option is to scatter all illustrations (black-and-white and color) throughout the book. The shorthand term for the method of printing that allows for this is 4/4 (printing in four colors on both sides of the sheet). In this method there are no restrictions on the placement of the reproductions; they may appear anywhere in the book. From everyone's point of view, this is a beautiful solution, but a very expensive one hardly ever used for dissertations.

The next option is to scatter color throughout the book but only on one side of the printing sheet. Unlike printing 4/4, the 4/1 method (printing one side of the sheet on four-color press and the other on a one-color press) places restrictions on which pages the color reproductions may appear. While this method gives the appearance of scattered color, it poses many disadvantages for the designer, and the reader may be slightly inconvenienced by color images that appear one or two pages after their text references.

Confining color reproductions to separate signatures (called inserts) is the most economical way to handle a modicum of color in a first book. Here the color is grouped on one or more signatures printed 4/4 and "inserted" at an appropriate place between signatures or wrapped around a signature so that eight pages of color appear at one place and the other eight pages sixteen pages later. For a 256-page book printed as sixteen 16-page signatures, the cost of printing all sixteen signatures 4/4 or 4/1 greatly exceeds the cost of printing fifteen signatures 1/1 and one signature 4/4.

ESTIMATE OF PHOTOGRAPHY AND PERMISSIONS COSTS

Granted, it is not wise to begin collecting and paying for images and reproduction rights until you have a publishing contract that confirms the number and kind of illustrations and sets out who is responsible for obtaining and paying for them. In particular, you surely do not want to start the meter ticking on the rental of your color transparencies, if any, until the publisher has called for them. But it is wise to do some preliminary probing that will give you an idea of the extent of the costs and as well may uncover problems while there is still time to resolve them or make substitutions.

Most museums and photo archives around the world will send you their schedule of fees if it is not already posted on their public Web site. Be sure you consult or ask for their "scholarly use" rate, which should differ appreciably from their rate for more commercial uses (such as postcards, calendars, films, and books with much larger print runs than yours). For the purpose of getting an estimate, specify a probable print run of twelve hundred copies, an approximate retail price of $50, English-language rights in North America and the United Kingdom (as many university presses have a branch or sales office in the UK), and a publication date—expressed as spring or fall of a certain year—fourteen months from the date you plan to deliver the final manuscript to the publisher.

It is important to investigate private collections early, not because their fees are likely to be exorbitant (they are usually very reasonable), but because, unlike institutions, private collectors may not have a stockpile of glossies or transparencies ready for lending. In fact, the only way to get a photograph may be to arrange for new photography, and that takes time as well as money.

If your dissertation covers twentieth-century art or the work of living artists, your photo and permissions bill and work may be compounded by the involvement of artist's rights groups such as ARS and VAGA in the United States and ADAGP and SPADEM in Europe. These groups representing artists and their estates exist to protect the copyright of artists and to ensure that the artists—and not just the owners of their work—are petitioned for permission to reproduce the artist's work and receive a copyright fee for such use. Each group publishes a list of artists and estates they represent and who must be approached through them; consult that list early and if possible meet or speak with a representative to determine what they are charging and how much of the work you can afford to include in your book. (As mentioned above, there is room for negotiation with these agencies, but you must approach them early, while there are alternatives.) Also, if you investigate all your sources at the outset and find some uncompromising lenders, there will still be time to make creative substitutions in your list of illustrations, avoiding where possible borrowing works from a museum or artist whose fees are out of your range.

Having a documented estimate of your total photo and permissions bill when you approach publishers will improve your chances of winning a modest advance (perhaps $1,000 or $1,500) toward your out-of-pocket photo expenses. It will also aid you in applying for departmental or university funding prior to or during the publication process. Even more important, it will convince you to use only as many illustrations as you really need. For you will discover immediately (and perhaps I can spare you some of the shock) that combined photo and reproduction fees for one hundred black-and-white illustrations are likely to be in neighborhood of $5,000. In metropolitan areas, that's several months' rent. For a twentieth-century subject, seventy-five black-and-white illustrations, and sixteen or twenty color plates, you might need to move back with your parents.

SPECIAL PROBLEMS

These problems are rare, but they do arise and sometimes in connection with dissertations. I can think of only two instances in my thirty-year career in scholarly publishing in which an artist and, separately, an artist's estate effectively blocked publication of a work that they found disagreeable by refusing to grant permission to print the illustrations. By not relinquishing a hold on the illustrations needed for the study, the artist/artist's estate engaged in a form of censorship, although they were acting within their legal rights. In another similar case, the book was published but sans illustrations in one section; in his preface the author apologized to readers for the visually barren chapter and tried to compensate in the body of the text with elaborate descriptions of the artist's work.

I mention this only because it is important to convey to prospective publishers any inkling you might have that such a problem exists for you. Perhaps the publisher will join your effort to combat the censorship or at least help find a creative solution. Then, too, the editor may decide not to pursue the project at all until the matter has been resolved.

SPECIAL EVENTS

On a more upbeat subject, editors should also be informed in book proposals about events that will coincide with the publication of the book that might have a salutary effect on the book's reception or sales. An exhibition, especially a traveling exhibition, that dovetails with the expected publication of your book would be of special interest to the editor and might be instrumental in getting your project into heaven. To a lesser degree, an upcoming anniversary of an artist's birth or death that is being marked by special publications or celebrations will be of interest to the editor.

SOURCES OF PUBLICATION FUNDING

Few categories of first books have a greater need for outside funding than those in the visual arts; at the same time, it is widely known and lamented that there are very few sources of such funding. Currently the Getty Grant Program is not awarding subsidies to individual books (it is hoped that this will change). Among the most familiar sources are the Barra Foundation, the College Art Association's Millard Meiss Fund, the Graham Foundation for Advanced Studies in the Fine Arts, the Samuel H. Kress Foundation, the Henry Luce Fund in American Art, the National Endowment for the Arts, the Judith Rothschild Foundation, and the Solow Foundation. Most do not accept applications for publication support from individuals (only from publishers with tax-exempt status), but they will accept inquiries from individuals. It is a very good idea to look into each of these in advance and report to your prospective publisher that such-and-such foundation is a possible source of funding for your book. In addition you should certainly scour the Foundation Center's comprehensive reference work, *The Foundation Directory, 2002* (David G. Jacobs, editor), or its online site at http://fconline.fdncenter.org, for other possible sources of funding for your topic or situation (being a resident of Maine, for example). Take note of foundations acknowledged in the literature on your topic, and contact those foundations for their guidelines. For more immediate help with out-of-pocket photography expenses, do not neglect your own department or university as a possible source for funding.

The purpose of sending you on all these missions is not, as you might believe, to make sure you are on your knees when it comes time to make the proposal. As time-consuming as these investigations may be, they are aimed at strengthening your proposal and your readiness for publication and at winning more than a glance from the art editor.

10

A SENSE OF PLACE

REGIONAL BOOKS

Ann Regan

We all know what regional books are. The section is usually right up front in the bookstore, not far from the cash register, beckoning impulse buyers. Its shelves are full of lavish picture books, hiking guides, state and local history, and—well, books published by regional publishers. A regional book is a book about the region.

But aren't most books about a region?

Regional is a publisher's marketing designation for books that are expected to sell mostly in one geographic area. Sometimes this categorization is indisputable. Books on a state's flora and fauna, bike trails and canoe routes, historic sites and place names will sell almost exclusively to tourists, residents of the state, and people who make a specialty of the specific topic. If a book has the name of a state in its title, booksellers outside that region will hesitate to carry it.

But this marketing label is an imperfect one. Other books on that regional shelf might appeal to anyone, anywhere: memoirs, essays, history books, books about architecture or popular culture or environmental issues. Booksellers place them there because they think that's where they will sell the most copies.

On the shelves in the rest of the store are thousands of wonderful books with vividly realized settings, characters who reflect local idiosyncrasies, and stories with universal appeal: Laurel Thatcher Ulrich's *A Midwife's Tale*; Maya Angelou's *I Know Why the Caged Bird Sings*; Russell Baker's *Growing Up*; Norman MacLean's *A River Runs through It*. Although each of these is set in a specific locale, none is seen as a regional book. They transcend "place" and speak to larger themes.

Many large publishers assert that they do not publish regional books. They do, however, publish good books that take place in specific areas, and they market them nationwide and—if they are doing a good job—with special attention to the book's home place. Conversely, many small publishers confidently identify themselves as regional presses. They know that the best books they publish transcend the region; if they are doing a good job, they also market their titles aggressively to the appropriate national audiences. And then there are presses, including many university presses, that publish books for a mix of national and regional markets. These university presses may offer an especially promising home for a dissertation on a regional topic, especially if they can position the book as a "crossover title"—a book that satisfies both scholarly and regional trade audiences. The publisher's demands on its author, however, are similar to those on authors of more trade-oriented books, as the press tries to enlarge that trade audience. If you plan to get a job teaching at a university, your advisors will tell you to publish for national distribution with the most prestigious scholarly press that you can—and they are right. The imprint of a large university or trade scholarly press is a kind of professional branding, and it will impress hiring committees and further your career.

So why pursue publication with a regional publisher at all? Your prospective colleagues may know that a university press, a museum, a historical society, or another regional institution has a respected booklist in your subject area. You may want to see your book marketed most heavily where it can make a difference. Perhaps you received guidance from the staff at an institution and you know that they will be particularly enthusiastic about producing and marketing your book. And then there is the most frustrating reason: your manuscript may have been rejected by your preferred university press. Although regional publishing may be your second choice, it's not a bad one. A good regional press may sell more copies of your book than that big scholarly press.

But don't assume that publishing with a regional press will be an easy fallback. We reject a lot of manuscripts too. Our publications are peer reviewed, and books must contribute valuable new insights and information. All of us have to make money by competing for space on that bookstore's bright, crowded regional shelf. Successful publishing starts with knowing the buyers. A dissertation published as a regional book will generally retain its audience of specialists. But careful revision may also attract the audience usually characterized as "educated lay readers": curious, amiable folks who have discretionary reading time and can be attracted to something that they find interesting. They are often well educated and sophisticated, interested in learning about the places where they live and expecting to have an intellectually rewarding experience.

Regional publishers face stiff competition for these discretionary readers, who can just as easily pick up a cookbook or the latest spy thriller. In the jargon of the business, this is trade publishing: selling books to a broad, nonspecialist market. Regional titles are sold in independent bookstores, regional sections of major chain stores, tourist shops, gift stores, and other specialty outlets. Their publishers must also have solid marketing connections to national wholesalers and chain stores in order to fill orders from booksellers within the area and, they hope, around the country.

Both nonprofit and decidedly commercial houses publish for regional markets. Presses may cover many disciplines or specialize in a few: natural history, history, biography, memoir, policy studies, anthropology, cultural studies, folklore, art, and architecture. But because each new title involves a risk of between $10,000 and $50,000, publishers need to shape their lists carefully.

The shaping of that list is both an economic decision and the source of a publisher's identity. A talented literary couple writes and publishes a few books on local literary figures, then decides to start publishing other people's manuscripts on artistic topics. A used bookstore owner publishes a few coffee-table books about his state and becomes a major publisher of natural history. Nonprofit institutions—mostly historical societies and museums—have publishing programs that further their mission and are also expected to make some money. Many university presses publish books about their states and regions, both as outreach to taxpayers and to generate revenue. The editors who acquire them must also think like trade publishers: regional books are generally expected to sell more and to have lower overall return rates than other titles on a university press's list. The more popular the region, the larger and more sophisticated the potential audience of lay readers: southern and western university presses, for example, have the enviable advantage of publishing for avocational readers who live all around the country.

The economics of regional publishers are like those of scholarly publishers. Both may print between eight hundred and three thousand copies of most revised dissertations and up to ten thousand copies of books with large potential audiences.

More than any other single item, your choice of a subject may decide whether a regional press can publish your work. Successful topics are easy to understand and have an immediate emotional appeal, while offering new intellectual insights. Topics in popular culture have strong interest: sports history, regional folklore and festivals, ethnic studies (e.g., Gary Ross Mormino's *Immigrants on the Hill: Italian-Americans in St. Louis, 1882–1982*). Books that deal with conflict and tragedy are often compelling: disaster stories, criminal history, civil unrest, Civil War history (Paul Hutton's *Phil Sheridan and His Army* and Stephen Hardin's *Texas Iliad: A Military History of the Texas Revolution*). Historical topics can immediately and clearly relate to people's lives in a region: aspects of the development of large cities, prominent industries, labor unions, and environmental issues (Joseph E. Taylor's *Making Salmon: An Environmental History of the Northwest Fisheries Crisis*). A dissertation may focus on a small town or lightly populated area to make a case study of a larger issue, but the study must have broad enough interest to attract readers outside that area (Paula M. Nelson's *After the West Was Won: Homesteaders and Town-Builders in Western South Dakota, 1900–1917*). Regional literature offers other options (Nicholas O'Connell's *On Sacred Ground: The Spirit of Place in Pacific Northwest Literature*).

Dissertations that focus on a subject of narrow interest—histories of small political movements, fine points of interpretation on topics that have been well covered—are far more difficult to publish. Is your topic reasonably easy to explain to someone over a beer? That's a good sign.

If you are using this book before starting your dissertation, you might call an acquiring editor and ask for an opinion about your project's publishability. (Even if you couch the question as a hypothetical, don't be surprised if you get a cautious response: weak writing can sink a good topic, and you are asking the editor to take yours on faith.) You can go prospecting for a topic in the manuscript and archival collections of universities, historical societies, or specialty libraries. Curators and librarians may be able to point out valuable and underused collections. You may write a successful book based on a collection of informative and beautiful photographs, richly detailed letters, or unexamined business records—and you may spot the topic for your second book as you research the first. Working with local primary sources can be tremendously exciting. You are uncovering the hidden stories of the place you are living in, finding the exotic aspects of a landscape that people take for granted.

As you do your research in these archives, you may meet other authors working on manuscripts for regional publishers. They are a wonderfully varied group. In recent years our press has published books by journalists, creative writing teachers, history professors, freelance writers, a public relations person, a truck driver, a retired electrician, a nurse, and a lawyer. A good regional author can be anyone with the eye for a good story, the imagination and energy to research it thoroughly, the creativity to know what it means, and the talent to write accurate, graceful, and informative prose.

Proposals from these prospective authors end up on the desks of regional acquisitions editors. Some acquiring editors, especially those at large university presses, say they will not accept submissions of unrevised dissertations. Don't let that stop you—but don't just drop your several-hundred-page behemoth in a box with a letter asking for an expression of interest. Write a letter that pitches the project, explains why it is of interest, identifies the main audience, and tells why it is appropriate for that publisher. Include an annotated copy of your contents page, revised to show what chapters will be dropped, what combined, and what themes will be further developed. Enclose a copy of your newly rewritten introduction and a sample chapter, but do not send the whole manuscript. With this framing, the editor can see the topic, your writing style, and some evidence that you can and will rework for publication. You may not get a contract, but the editor can at least give you an informed indication of the press's interest.

WRITING FOR A REGIONAL AUDIENCE

A local topic doesn't mean that a manuscript is automatically of interest to a regional publisher. It must also be well written. You undoubtedly noticed the hallmarks of good writing among the scores of books you read as you researched your dissertation: clear prose, cogent explication, careful pacing, respect for the reader, and a modest, un-self-conscious authorial voice. Your new goal is to do all this in sixty thousand to one hundred thousand words, including footnotes.

An editor's first advice to an author revising a dissertation is simple. Delete the review of the literature and trim the footnotes. (In fact, a publisher may ask you to drop the footnotes entirely.) Read *The Elements of Style* by William Strunk and E. B. White and follow its rules. When in doubt about a sentence, read it aloud and revise it until it works.

But clear writing that is technically correct will only get you so far. A greater challenge is to deliver the direct, confident storytelling that draws readers in, especially those who are not used to reading academic studies. You must keep your eye on them, know where they are at all times, and be solicitous of their happiness. They can be skittish, and they can bolt at any moment.

It can be difficult to know how much context to provide. Some people know more about their home place than others—and some just think they do. Reasonably literate Americans may have forgotten what they once knew about the Civil War, but Civil War buffs will be annoyed if they are lectured on the importance of Antietam. To steer between the two audiences, provide some background, in subordinate clauses, as if it is a gentle reminder. Assume that your reader is as smart as you are. Some writers find it helpful to imagine they are writing for a specific person: their favorite uncle, their terrific tenth-grade English teacher, another writer whose work they admire—some no-nonsense critic who has good judgment and knows them well enough to respond honestly.

Pause periodically to provide summary and comment—the interpretation—when readers are ready to understand the meaning of a story. Go light on theory, except as necessary for interpretation. Play up your first-person quotes and primary sources, taking advantage of the emotional immediacy that eyewitnesses provide. Avoid long block quotes, which readers tend to skip.

Not all books need illustrations, and not all illustrations will reproduce clearly. If it is appropriate for your subject, your proposal will be stronger if you can provide copies of clear, interesting photographs that help make your point. Keep photocopies, with their origins clearly labeled. If the book is illustrated, the work of tracking down copy prints or scans will be yours.

As you revise, remember the main question: What is this book about? Keep the focus on the larger story by including a point only if it tells the reader something essential, only if it moves your argument along. Edit yourself ruthlessly. You are competing for the attention of people who are constantly told complete stories in fifteen-second commercials. They know that reading is a more intensive activity, but they need to know that you are respecting their time, giving them necessary information, and not trying to show everything you have learned. Remember, they are reading your book by choice, and their patience is not infinite.

PUBLICATION

When your revision is done, you will probably be fed up with your own work. Fortunately, the review process takes an astonishing length of time, even at a regional publishing house, and you may have an opportunity to forget entire paragraphs that you memorized while rewriting.

Regional publishers are usually too small to assign an editor to acquisitions work alone, and work on books already in production pushes hard against work on prospective manuscripts for two or three seasons hence. After the acquiring editor finds some time to spend with the manuscript and confirms that the topic matches the list, the level of writing is acceptable, and the book would be reasonably marketable, he or she sends it to an anonymous expert or two for review. The reviewers may raise questions that you need to address, but a manuscript is usually accepted or rejected at this stage.

If it is accepted without a call for major revisions, celebrate but prepare yourself: the text will come back to you for careful attention after it is edited. After all your hard work, it can be a challenge to accept someone else's mucking about with your prose. But an editor who has been working with regional books for a while has a kind of expertise that can save you from embarrassing mistakes.

Editing involves an unusual intellectual intimacy. Mark Twain, or perhaps Ernest Hemingway—the quote is variously attributed—supposedly said that editors like the taste of the water better after they have pissed in it. Ivan Doig says that being edited is like being nibbled to death by ducks. I prefer to think of being edited as deep body massage: it may not be entirely comfortable, but if you relax into it, you'll feel great about it when it is over. Don't allow your editor to insert errors or gut your arguments, but stay receptive to suggested changes. It may be the most honest feedback you will ever get.

Regional publishers will work hard to sell your book in a U.S. marketplace jammed with over 115,000 new titles each year. Because smaller houses publish fewer books, they can pay more attention to each one, but they may employ just one person to handle sales, publicity, and exhibits. Larger houses have more staff members, but they divide their time among more titles. In either case, because the regional book's main audience lives within an identifiable geographic area, it is easier to reach them. If your book has enough popular appeal, you will probably be asked to do book signings. There is a direct correlation between an author's spirited involvement in marketing her own book and that book's regional success. Readings and signings tend to draw small crowds, but don't be discouraged. Be cheerful and make friends with the store's staff, who will be selling your book. The publicity for the event, seen by all those people who didn't show up, expands the awareness of your book. You may be asked to do local television and radio talk shows—our authors have done lively call-ins at 1:00 A.M.—and even state fair appearances.

If your book does not inspire a local media frenzy, don't worry. You still have readers, and they are an impressive bunch. Nobody makes us buy and read books about our home place. We do not have to keep up with the literature, we are not expected to drop names of authors in casual conversation. We buy regional books because we like learning more about something we already know. We enjoy seeing familiar landscapes in unfamiliar times, taking intellectual and emotional journeys through a well-known place. These books surprise us with insights about ourselves, and they help us understand the odd habits of our neighbors. Beautiful picture books evoke powerful memories, insightful studies tie our lives to national and global history, literary memoirs temporarily give us new identities in nearby neighborhoods. Well written, beautifully produced regional books provide context for the toughest issues our communities face; they make us more empathetic, energetic, and informed citizens; and they help us make better decisions about how we live in a place.

If you publish your work with a regional press, you may experience the immense pleasure of writing for people who will be delighted to hear what you tell them. Your readers will recognize themselves in what you write and understand your research in ways you cannot envision. You can change the way people look at their world.

11

MAKING A DIFFERENCE

PROFESSIONAL PUBLISHING

Johanna E. Vondeling

When I applied for a job in the editorial department of Jossey-Bass in the late 1990s, I had never heard of "professional publishing." I had worked in a variety of publishing capacities: in addition to writing a dissertation, I'd worked for newspapers, college and high school textbook publishers, and scholarly and literary journals. Professional publishing, however, was unfamiliar territory. I studied Jossey-Bass's backlist and assured myself it couldn't be that different from other kinds of editing. In some ways I was right, as there are key convergences between scholarly, textbook, technical, literary, and trade publishing. However, I've also learned that professional publishing is its own kind of animal, with unique demands and rewards for author and reader alike. Professional publications translate challenging ideas into forms that are useful and appealing to the people best positioned to put those ideas into practice. In this way, professional publications have the somewhat rare distinction of using research to make a practical difference.

For first-time authors hoping to publish books based on their graduate work, this chapter explains professional publishing as a means to that end. It explains both how professional publishing differs from other venues and some of the editorial and economic considerations that motivate acquisition editors who work in the field. Finally, it provides guidance on how to craft an appealing proposal, how to work with a publisher during the development process, and what steps you can take to increase your publication's chances of reaching a wide audience.

WHAT IS PROFESSIONAL PUBLISHING?

Professional publishing is, at its most basic, knowledge transfer. While this is true of all kinds of writing, professional publishing distinguishes itself as the effort to translate theory and best practices into language that is accessible to the practitioner. Writers of professional texts collect thoughtful research and behavior models from organizational settings and translate these data into useful guidance for the reader. As a genre, professional publishing is defined less by the nature of its content than by its practical benefits to those working in the field. The audience is neither the dissertation advisor looking for evidence of how much the student knows, nor the general public looking for entertainment, nor the die-hard academic with an insatiable desire for knowledge. Instead, the audience is practitioners—individuals with varying degrees of academic training, working in specific professions, such as business, psychology, or education—who are looking for concrete guidance that will help them perform more effectively in the workplace. These professionals have specialized skills and experience. They have concrete agendas and are deeply committed to their work. Successful writers understand that the key to a strong publication is to respect professionals' commitment to their goals, to understand "what's on the daily minds of those individuals, what kinds of issues, dilemmas, problems or situations these individuals face that this new information could help solve."[1]

THE CHALLENGES AND REWARDS OF PROFESSIONAL WRITING FOR ACADEMICS

As "useful information for the specialized professional," professional publishing represents a sizable challenge for the writer-academic hoping to publish research that has first been collected and organized in a university context. All writers hoping to provide thought leadership for professional audiences through their publications must have an unusual degree of empathy for the demands of the working professional. Writers trained in an academic environment face the additional task of overcoming some of the hard-earned training acquired in graduate school. They must learn to quell their natural instincts to share all they know and must prioritize on the grounds of what works rather than what can be most astutely proven true. This is hard work for academics, and work that offers no guaranteed financial compensation.

The rewards of successful professional writing, however, can

1. André L. Delbecq, "Publishing as Knowledge Transfer: An Interview with Lynn D. W. Luckow, President and CEO of Jossey-Bass, Inc.," in *Impact Analysis: How Research Can Enter Application and Make a Difference*, ed. Laurie Larwood (Mahwah, N.J.: Lawrence Erlbaum, 1999), 47–53.

often be more satisfying than those of scholarly publishing in that such publications grant writers the rare opportunity to see their research and ideas put to practical use. Effective professional publications, for example, can help businesses observe higher ethical standards, help psychologists treat patients more humanely, promote more effective health care delivery, or facilitate a fairer distribution of wealth between the private and public sectors. In short, professional writing can help promote real change in the real world. For academics who may have lamented the sorry state of the world while fretting over the solipsistic dangers of their ivory tower work, professional writing is a way to make a quantifiable difference.

For academic writers hoping to effect change in practice through their writing, professional publishing means developing some new communication skills. As Jossey-Bass's former president and CEO has observed, one of the greatest impediments to providing a bridge between theory and practice "is the graduate school experience, whereby a particular style or writing is encouraged and fostered . . . [where] the focus is more on methodology and the links to existing theory." In academia, "the focus is on subject matter versus situation matter and the communication is to other theoreticians and researchers rather than a translation to those in practice."[2] In the professional arena, by contrast, information is most useful when it can be effectively and efficiently applied to a particular situation—when readers can use the research and models to improve their own work or their own organizations. For example, Diana Newman's 2001 publication for fundraising professionals, *Opening Doors: Pathways to Diverse*

2. Ibid., 50.

Donors, began as an academic research report observing philanthropic practices in communities of color. While the report's raw data would have had only limited appeal within the professional community, the author refocused and expanded the report's content to underscore practical lessons fundraisers could learn from the research. Each chapter clearly identifies the implications for professionals and suggests action steps that can improve an organization's performance. Newman's book translates theory into practice: it uses careful research to help professional fundraisers achieve organizational goals—in this case, raise more money to fund programs. Similarly, Elizabeth Tisdell's *Exploring Spirituality and Culture in Adult and Higher Education* began as a qualitative research study but underwent significant expansion and restructuring. Rather than simply observing or quantifying the spiritual and cultural factors that influence adult learning, the final publication suggests specific strategies educators can use to promote social transformation by applying this information in the classroom.

The litmus test of usefulness leads professional publishers to evaluate the merits of proposals first and foremost on the grounds of "need." The first question professional book editors ask of a proposal is "Do readers need to have this information in order to perform their jobs better?" (In this context, "need to have" is juxtaposed with "nice to know.") For similar reasons, professional publishers tend to decline works of advocacy intended to tell professionals what they "should" be doing or thinking. I am not the only editor who has been forced—regrettably—to cancel a project when it became evident that the authors' primary goal was to change readers' thinking on some controversial political issue, rather than to show readers key strategies for achieving the agendas they labored long and hard to set for themselves. Works of advocacy, like works of basic research and pure theory, have an important place in the publishing world, and all professional publishers respect and support the goals of such publications. Ultimately, however, professional publishers adopt practical resources for receptive, rather than reluctant, readers. These readers know where they want to go; professional publications show them the way.

For academic writers accustomed to constructing arguments that are valorized on the grounds of novelty or intellectual incisiveness, or because they provocatively urge readers to reconsider their fundamental positions on complex theoretical issues, prioritizing the practical necessity of information is a significant shift. This is not to say that professional publishers and the readers of professional books do not prize innovation; on the contrary, they know well that new, exciting best practices are constantly evolving. However, first and foremost, professional readers seek information that has immediate value and applications, information that will lead readers, not just to think differently, but more importantly to act differently within the professional setting.

WHO IS THE PROFESSIONAL READER?

As with all writing, the question of audience is key. While it is always dangerous to generalize, professional readers can be said to differ from students or dissertation advisors or readers of novels in that they are looking for specific information that can be applied to specific, work-related situations. Such readers assuredly have a fair degree of natural curiosity about the subject at hand, but they probably also have full-time jobs outside the academy, which limit their time for abstract thinking. Often, editors of professional books must steer authors away from providing lengthy theoretical and methodological background and historical orientation, since most professional readers expect authors to distill key points for them. For example, an academic researcher studying the social sector probably knows the tortured evolution of a particular line of thinking regarding the rise of the current nonprofit board model; however, practicing board members probably don't need to know this information in order to engineer effective strategic planning within an agency. Readers of professional books tend to favor discussions of principles supported by occasional examples over collections of case studies that require them to extrapolate practical applications for their own situations. Illuminating examples of key principles are invaluable, but they must be used to support preestablished arguments. Given the time constraints of their work, readers of professional books consistently prefer direct advice over hedgy hypotheses, however thought-provoking such speculations might be.

Readers of professional books, however, are not a monolithic mass. They have varying degrees of experience and educational training in their field, and the professions they serve are remarkably varied. Writing for this audience requires authors to have a strong working knowledge of the specific field in question, since practitioners can be skeptical of academia and pride themselves on knowledge gained from experience. All readers of professional books, however, have a strong distaste for jargon and expect writers to use language that is transparent and democratic.

CONVENTIONS AND TONE IN PROFESSIONAL WRITING

Given the prioritization of need in professional writing, it should come as little surprise that such publications adhere to few conventions. In addition to the body of the text, professional publications may or may not contain any of the following elements: foreword, preface, acknowledgments, introduction, conclusion or afterword, list of references, bibliography, and resources. No editor I know dogmatically insists on the inclusion of any of these elements; instead, editors are inclined to allow the needs of the audiences and the nature of the content to determine their value in the publication.

While no specific generic elements are de rigueur in professional writing, professional writers trained in academia can expect that their editors will press them to provide more explicit signposts than are generally found in scholarly writing. In academia, revealing your thesis in the first paragraph can be considered hasty or, worse, gauche. In professional writing, the writer should be explicit about the benefits of the work to the reader and should do so as early as possible. Among key signposts, the table of contents and preface are arguably the most critical. The table of contents serves two purposes: it predicts the arc of information contained in the work, and it functions as a key marketing tool in catalogs, reviews, and online venues. In short, it is the most efficient indicator of what a reader can hope to gain from reading the work. For these reasons, the logical progression indicated in the organization must be self-evident, and the language used to describe that progression must be as transparent as possible. The preface serves to frame the scope, set the tone, and establish the benefits of the work for the reader. In my experience, the most effective prefaces (1) state the purpose of the work and why it was written, (2) identify the audience, (3) explain how the author expects the book to be used, and (4) provide a preview of the content by summarizing the goals of the succeeding chapters. While some authors find this guidance too prescriptive, others discover that the simple act of drafting a preface helps them to clarify their goals and strengthen their organization. Frequent subheadings are also a common feature of professional publications.

Most editors of professional books are similarly flexible with respect to tone. Again, the needs of the audience and the exigencies of content are more important in successful professional publishing than any universal conventions. A handbook of best hiring practices for academic deans, for example, probably warrants a greater degree of formality than a beginner's guide to grant seeking for youth groups. Writers should rest assured, however, that the academic values of professional distance and objectivity need not be sacrificed at the altar of professional publishing. It's fair to say that authors with consulting backgrounds generally employ a more conversational tone than their peers in academia; however, that is not to say that consultant-authors are consistently more successful than tenured professors. As Elizabeth Rankin instructs authors in *The Work of Writing:* "Although finding a voice may entail having the courage to challenge the more conservative conventions of academic writing—conventions that encourage passive verbs and forbid first-person pronouns, for instance—it need not be as difficult as it seems. Finding a voice is mostly a matter of developing an ear for language and having the confidence to integrate who you are as a person with who you are as a professional."[3] To Rankin's solid advice, I would add that, ultimately, the question of voice in professional publishing is about finding the right blend of what's comfortable for the author and what's right for the reader.

CRAFTING YOUR PROPOSAL

Given the important distinctions between the goals of academic and professional writing, the dissertation submitted as defended to a professional publisher is virtually guaranteed to be declined. In all cases, the most practical first step is to research current publishers and identify those who have a history of publishing for the specific professional audience your research will interest. These include both commercial publishing houses and professional associations with in-house publishing programs, such as the Modern Language Association, BoardSource, and the American Psychological Association. In all cases, you should obtain their proposal guidelines and frame your proposal according to the key questions the publisher has outlined.

Some general rules, however, can guide those seeking to publish for professional audiences, regardless of the specific subsectors individual publishers serve. If you have an idea for a writing project that you feel could appeal to professional readers, first identify the "need-to-have" element in your work. The fact that no one has previously published a book on a given subject is not evidence of need. Likewise, asserting that a proposed publication

3. Elizabeth Rankin, *The Work of Writing: Insights and Strategies for Academics and Professionals* (San Francisco: Jossey Bass, 2001), 54.

222 / Johanna E. Vondeling

will "contribute to the literature" will not convince an editor that professional readers need this information to excel in their work. Instead, begin by identifying a need in the community you hope your publication will serve. What goals does that community have that are currently not being met? (Remember that this is different from identifying goals that you think that community *should* have.) Are there gaps in training? professional development? organizational knowledge and practice?

Next, explain how your research will help address the needs of the community. Effective professional publications often devote some energy to explaining the roots of the problem, but chances are that readers committed to a particular profession are already well aware of the individual and organizational shortcomings that hinder their community, so reiterating these problems is merely preaching to the choir. While your research may have indicated problems in abstract elements like organizational culture, your goal is to identify specific strategies for addressing those problems.

Identifying the needs of the community at hand necessarily means identifying the needs and interests of your individual target readers. A common misstep among would-be authors is to attempt to convince editors that their project will appeal to "everyone." In fact, the broader the audience, the less likely the information is to be "need-to-have." Identifying a host of possible readers will only cast doubt on the essential value of your research. A body of research may well appeal to a variety of workers in the professional community, but writing for "everyone" will inevitably result in advice that either is trying too hard to appeal to too many readers or is too generic to be much use to any of them. Instead, choose a primary audience within a specific profession (e.g., human resource professionals or academic deans), as well as a few potential secondary audiences. Editors also find it helpful when authors further identify the professional experience of the target audience and explain the knowledge base they are assuming among their readers.

Editors evaluating proposals for professional books are also always eager to learn about competing publications. As mentioned above, the fact that no other publisher has ever entered this arena is not always welcome news to editors. In addition to casting doubt on the "need-to-have" value of the work, the absence of comparable track records indicates a greater level of risk for the publisher. In any event, it's highly unlikely that no one has ever published on your chosen subject, at least in some capacity. Your proposal will garner closer attention if you highlight how your book is similar to and different from competing publications. In addition to researching competing publications at the library, visit local bookstores and online retailers like Amazon.com to learn more about the competition for your project, and include this information in your proposal package. (As a side note, reports that are distributed free are not technically competing publications, and your editor will view circulation figures for such publications with considerable skepticism.)

As publishers like proven track records, published authors are generally more appealing than novices. Do include information about your previous publications, but recognize that editors will be evaluating your samples on the basis of your ability to write for a professional audience. (For this reason, a jargon-filled academic study might not help your case, so choose wisely.) Lack of publishing experience, however, is not an insurmountable barrier to securing a contract, as long you have both a strong proposal and other means of proving your potential and value to the publisher.

MAKING YOURSELF ATTRACTIVE TO PROFESSIONAL PUBLISHERS

First and foremost, it helps to remember that commercial professional publishers are businesses, not charitable enterprises or educational nonprofits. The books editors adopt for professional audiences must not only cover the ever-increasing expenses of development, production, marketing, and distribution but also make a profit. Authors who understand the economic considerations influencing commercial publishers are generally more attractive to editors and, ultimately, more widely read than those who dismiss marketplace concerns. Nonprofit publishers who have alternative sources of revenue (such as funding from foundations) sometimes have more latitude to produce works that lack broad commercial appeal in the professional arena; however, nonprofit publishers are also often smaller than their commercial competitors and are likely to have both fewer resources to devote to marketing their publications and weaker relationships with major distribution outlets like retail stores and online vendors.

While the most important adoption criteria for commercial professional publishers are the quality and "need-to-have" nature of a project's content, authors themselves are critical considerations. Given the ever-narrowing margins in all sectors of the publishing industry, publications rarely succeed on the merits of good ideas alone. Professional publishers cannot survive without authors who are prominent public figures within their respective professional communities, and an author's "platform" is an essential component of any promising publishing proposal. Given the choice between a retiring academic whose sole interaction with the target audience is a course or two each semester and a consultant who spends much of the year on the road cultivating a large client base and promoting best practices to potential customers, the publisher will invariably choose the active consultant.

Aspiring professional writers can enhance their appeal to publishers by cultivating a strong, multifaceted platform. In addition to pursuing public speaking engagements in the private sector or at professional conferences, start building a base of contacts that can be leveraged to help promote your book once it is published. Contribute to the publications that serve this professional community, such as newsletters and membership magazines of professional organizations, not just to the scholarly publications that study these professions. If possible, get appointed or elected to leadership positions within professional associations, since such work will not only increase your knowledge of professionals' needs but also establish links to key marketing opportunities down the road. Pursue media attention whenever possible.

Strong author platforms pay dividends through higher sales and, ultimately, greater impact within the professional community. One of our most successful authors received her graduate degree in theology but now makes her living as a fundraising consultant. She is in high demand as a speaker and presenter and has provided training and consultation throughout the United States and abroad. In addition to writing five professional titles, she is the co-publisher of a bimonthly newsletter, has contributed to dozens of books and periodicals, and distributes a monthly e-mail newsletter. She promotes her books through each of these venues, and her aggressive approach to marketing means that her books are widely read in the fundraising community. Most importantly, the research and principles she presents in her publications have influenced an entire generation of fundraisers. Her advice has dramatically improved their ability to raise money for their organizations, thus advancing those groups' ability to promote social change.

CHOOSING YOUR FORMAT

Within professional publishing, format is increasingly varied. Most projects developed within academic environments tend to be straight, text-based treatises with some charts and other graphical data for statistical support. Workers in professional communities, however, may be looking for knowledge transfer in other formats. Given the practical orientation of professional workers, many actually prefer to receive information in ready-to-use formats rather than as expository narrative. In an effort to serve these professionals, publishers encourage authors to "think format-independent," to be flexible and creative when considering the best vehicle for their research.

To determine the most appropriate (and most needed) format for your project, survey the professionals you expect to find your material useful, and use their feedback to guide the development of your project. For example, consider whether the true need-to-have nature of your information might most effectively be presented in a workbook format that would enable readers to apply the advice directly to their own experiences. If your project has potential practical applications within a training environment, consider proposing an electronic component that might make your materials easy to reproduce within an institutional or retreat setting. Ultimately, your publication will have greater success—greater impact in the community—if your publication's format meets the particular needs of your audience's workplace environment.

WORKING WITH YOUR EDITOR

A good editor is an essential component of any successful professional publishing project. While your editor probably won't share your depth of technical expertise, he or she can be an invaluable guide and champion for your project within the publishing company. When initiating contact with an editor, be sure to establish clear, common goals for the project, and don't hesitate to ask questions. Good editors should speak articulately about their own company's goals and about how your project fits with those goals. Good editors also identify the publisher's commitment to the project (before and after publication) and are straightforward about marketing and deadline expectations. If you are negotiating your contract directly with your editor, you can expect him or her to be honest and forthright about the terms; however, don't expect your editor to act as your legal advisor. If, after discussing the contract carefully, you still have reservations, consult a lawyer.

DEVELOPING YOUR PROJECT

Once you have secured a contract for your professional book, the real work begins. In most cases, an editor commits to a project on the grounds of a sensible-sounding table of contents and a few sample chapters. (In some cases, editors looking for adoption advice also send proposals out for external review.) Depending on your disposition, you may choose a high level of collaboration with your editor throughout the construction of the draft, but typically the most intensive development stage occurs after the submission of a full manuscript. Professional works are designed to convey specialized information to a specialized audience, and it is rare that an editor possesses both the organizational and business skills required to be an editor *and* the specialized knowledge required to fill the needs of a professional audience. For this reason, the external review process is an essential phase in the development of any professional work.

At Jossey-Bass, the review process usually involves the solicitation of three or four professional peers who provide feedback anonymously. We request a three- to four-page review evaluating both the project's overall merits and the quality of individual chapters. We seek reviewers both from the academic community and from the professional community the book is intended to serve. We encourage authors to suggest reviewers, but we tend to avoid relying solely on the author's suggestions, since personal familiarity can inhibit constructive feedback.

In most cases, authors receive blinded reviews along with a letter from the editor synthesizing reviewer recommendations and arbitrating points of reviewer dispute. The editor's role here is to distill the key recommendations for revision and to provide guidance based on the editor's own knowledge of what constitutes a promising professional publication. While editors often defer to reviewers on questions of technical merit, they provide important guidance about framing, format, and packaging—guidance the author is unlikely to receive from content experts. As likely generalists, editors can be especially helpful in evaluating a draft's ability to signpost key arguments and to speak to practitioners in clear and persuasive language.

MARKETING PROFESSIONAL PUBLICATIONS

Every publisher dreams of the need-to-have book that sells itself. Unfortunately, most professional titles require intensive marketing by the publisher and author alike. Unlike trade publishing, which is driven largely by advertising and publicity to generalized audiences, professional publishing relies heavily on direct marketing to specialized readers. The larger professional publishers work with major retailers like Barnes and Noble and online retailers like Amazon.com to secure real and virtual "shelf space" for their professional titles. However, given that these titles are designed for specialized (i.e., narrow) audiences, getting a retailer's attention for a professional book can be difficult. To overcome this challenge, successful professional publishers rely heavily on marketing strategies like catalogs and e-mail advertising that enable them to speak directly to these specialized audiences. Authors can increase their appeal to publishers and help market their books directly to these audiences by collecting and sharing mailing lists of their contacts and clients.

Marketing to professional associations is also a key building block in the foundation of any successful promotional effort. Professional associations are increasingly important customer groups, both because of their missions and because of their size. Most professional associations have included the professional development of their members as part of their organizational goals. And, on a purely economic level, it's more cost-effective to promote a title to a single organization with ten thousand members than to mail individual catalogs to ten thousand professionals. If they're committed to helping their members, professional associations have a vested interest in learning more about new publications and other resources and in sharing these tools with their members. In some cases, professional associations adopt publications as benefits of membership or resell titles to members, thus ensuring significant sales. Authors can help publishers promote their books to professional associations by identifying promising groups, speaking at annual and local conferences, and serving in professional capacities within those associations.

Professional publishers' most important marketing assets, however, are authors themselves. Through their speaking appearances and interactions with clients, authors spur word-of-mouth promotion and garner general goodwill toward the publication. Charismatic authors who speak frequently likewise attract media attention. In addition to reinforcing the publisher's own marketing efforts, such public appearances also offer authors the opportunity to boost sales (and personal income) by reselling books at their speaking engagements.

Professional writing requires researchers and scholars trained in academia to assume a new identity: translator. To provide information that is truly accessible to the reader, this alter ego must guide both the goals of the publication and the way the author communicates information. The demands of translation mean privileging the situational needs of the reader above all else and "defining what you have to say and saying it clearly, concisely, and early enough that the reader cannot miss the point."[4] The rewards can be gratifyingly concrete. Writers who successfully translate their knowledge of a subject or discipline into thoughtful guidance that improves practice have the rare pleasure of seeing all they know put to good use.

4. Ibid., 26.

THE TICKING CLOCK

Beth Luey

Perhaps the greatest problem young scholars face in revising their dissertations is the shortage of time. Tenure review comes up surprisingly fast. Postdoctoral fellowships that free up a year or two for research and writing are hard to get, and part of those years must often be devoted to finding a job for the following year. Those with teaching posts must cope with new responsibilities as teachers and colleagues, along with the responsibility to publish. Department chairs and tenure committees may expect them to publish articles along the way, which they casually say could be plucked from the dissertation, ignoring the fact that book publishers discourage such scavenging.

Getting a book or a substantial number of articles written under the gun is difficult. The keys to success—in addition to good brains and good scholarly training, which you obviously have—are planning the discipline. "Planning Tools," at the end of this book, will help. If you are aiming for book publication, a sound approach is to start with the date by which you must have a completed, accepted manuscript. For journal articles, look at how many you are expected to have accepted by that date. Then count backwards, allowing at least a year for submission and revision of a book, and various periods for the writing and acceptance of articles. That gives you about four years to write a book, and six months to a year per article. If you are beginning with your dissertation, you have most or all of the basic research done, so that is actually plenty of time. A dissertation completed in the spring can be set aside during the summer. Spend those months getting ready to teach and reading good books that can serve as inspiration and models. Being well prepared for your classes will prevent your first semester of teaching from overwhelming you. If you do not finish until late summer, you'll have to use the time while your committee is reading to prepare for classes.

Once you begin teaching, it will seem as though you cannot possibly get any writing done, but you can if you develop discipline and good habits. Write for an hour every day. You won't always be writing something that will end up in your finished publication, but make sure you write. This may mean getting up early, writing during a free hour between classes (with your door firmly shut), or writing before bedtime. (I don't recommend this because you're tired, and writing doesn't help you sleep.) It doesn't matter when you write, or where, or what—at least at first. Just make sure you build time for writing into every day. Set the time aside, and make it inviolable. If you write regularly, it becomes easier and more enjoyable. Always stop writing in the middle of a paragraph or even in the middle of a sentence. That way, when you come back to the work it is easy to get started and you are not facing the dreaded blank page. When you finish a chapter or large section, be sure to write a paragraph that either starts the next section or reminds you what will be in it. Revising what you wrote the day before does not count. The hour is for actual writing. When you finish a chapter, you should let it sit for at least a few days before revising. Time spent revising whole chapters can be counted as writing time.

Look for ways to free up your summers and winter breaks. Apply for research grants. If teaching summer school means the difference between paying your rent and not paying it, then teach summer school. But if it means only the difference between a new car and putting up with the old one for two or three years, pass it up. Learn to say no to things that do not matter as much to your career as research and teaching. Review only books that you need to read. If necessary, seek the protection of your chair or a mentor from demanding committee assignments. Some departments give junior faculty a semester free from teaching, or a reduced load, so that they can write. If you are fortunate enough to have this opportunity, choose your semester carefully so that the time will be most productive.

In addition to your daily writing time, set aside a longer block of time once a week—perhaps on a day when you do not teach, or on the weekend. Four hours is plenty; few people can write productively any longer than that. You may find that two blocks of two hours work better. Again, make the time regular and inviolable.

Everyone works differently. Some people write sentence by sentence. Others think out chapters in their heads so that when they sit down at the keyboard, whole paragraphs flow from their fingers. You know best how you work (and how you procrastinate), so you can come up with a plan that suits your most productive style.

"Useful Reading" lists books that may help you structure the time for carrying out your revisions. "Planning Tools" offers a worksheet and a list of brief writing tasks that will provide structure. Here is one plan for someone who works best on a regular schedule and who cannot stand working down to the wire. During the first semester of teaching, try to block out a plan for revising. Envision the book you want to write, and figure out what you need to do to get there. This is an extremely important step. If you do not have a clear goal and plan, your work is likely to be random and inefficient. Whether you work best from a detailed summary, an outline, a diagram, or some other sort of intellectual map, take the time to plan thoroughly and record your plans in a form that you can use. You will probably modify the plan as you go along, but you need something to start with.

During the second semester, remove from the dissertation what you do not need and plan any additional research you will have to do. This planning should include ordering microfilm, interlibrary loan books, or equipment you will need so that you can get some real work done during the summer. It should also include applying for fellowships (but check deadlines because some are due in the fall). Writing fellowship applications counts as part of your daily writing. It also helps you articulate exactly what you are doing. If you are reasonably confident about how your book will turn out, you can write a prospectus and begin sending it out to publishers. If not, this can wait.

The summer and the following fall semester can be used to do the research and reading required. Over the winter break, you can begin to write seriously. You will undoubtedly find that you need to do more reading and research, but you should get started on the writing. During the spring, continue your research and writing. You may be able to write an article based on material you won't be using in the book, or perhaps on something you have turned up during your research. But whatever you are working on, write every day.

The next summer is the opportunity to get a large chunk of writing done—enough to submit to a publisher, if you have not already gotten started on this. By fall, you should have an appealing prospectus and a couple of chapters to send out. You may even have an article or two added to your curriculum vitae. ("Useful Reading" suggests books you can consult on writing the prospectus, selecting possible publishers, and following submission procedures.)

Your third year is the time to finish writing. Remember that if you write only one page a day, you will have written a good-sized book in a year. Since you have already completed part of the book, a page a day will easily do the trick—with time to spare for revisions. At least one publisher will have expressed interest in your work by now (you may even have an advance contract), so you can send it off. While you're waiting, work on articles, jot down notes for additions and revisions, and try not to worry. This schedule allows for slippage and gives you plenty of time to revise in response to peer reviewers' comments.

If you are writing articles, you have a good deal more flexibility, but you need to be just as diligent about keeping up the pace. When you finish an article, there is an enormous temptation to kick back and take it easy until it is accepted. You need to resist this temptation, because you must begin at least thinking about the next article almost immediately. It is also possible that you won't hear from the journal for quite a while (or even that the article will be rejected or require extensive revision), and there isn't that much time to waste. By all means, declare a work-free weekend, but don't take a month off.

All of this may sound fairly grim. In fact, you will find that being productive reduces anxiety considerably and allows you to have more fun in your well-earned leisure time, scarce though that may be. You will also find that writing regularly makes you write more easily. By the time you finish your first book or set of articles, you should begin to find writing enjoyable and even, at times, relaxing. Many people discover that writing actually releases tension, because it organizes and expresses material that is otherwise a sort of chaotic mass in your brain. I'm not sure that neurologists would accept that explanation, but it's a good description of the feeling.

Many people worry about writer's block, many more than actually experience it. True writer's block—the kind of anxiety that prevents the sufferer from putting words on a page, or keeping them there, or even sitting down to write—is mercifully rare. If you experience it, you should seek help from a psychologist. What most people call writer's block is a variety of minor intellectual or procedural disturbances.

One variety is the inability to get started on a project. It usually happens when the subject remains inchoate: you aren't ready to write because you don't know exactly what you're trying to say. There are three approaches to this problem. The first is to spend time talking to yourself, aloud or silently, about what you're trying to write. Tell yourself the story. At some point in the conversation, your material should take shape sufficiently to give you a place to start—a topic sentence or paragraph. A second approach is simply to admit that you don't know where to start, pick an arbitrary place, and start writing. You may end up throwing away what you write, or putting it in the middle, but at least you will have started. A third approach is to write a formal, boring introductory paragraph of the kind you were taught to write in freshman composition: Here's what I'm going to say. It may be wrong, and even if it's right you will end up throwing it away, but—again—you've gotten started.

Some people find themselves unable to write in the middle of a project. If this is caused by doubts about what you have written so far, ask yourself whether you're worrying about something major and substantive that will affect the rest of the project. If not, set the doubts aside and forge ahead. If so, take a day off and then reread what you have written—not for style and small things but for the quality of the argument and the evidence. If there is a problem, fix it. If not, go back to where you were and get started.

A third variety is the inability to stop fussing about details. You cannot move forward because there are so many little things wrong with what you have already written that you feel compelled to clean them up. This isn't writer's block but a form of procrastination: it's much easier to fix what's written than to create something new. Fight the temptation.

Procrastination, of course, takes many forms. The quality of life in our house rises considerably when I'm having trouble writing. The house is cleaner, there's homemade bread, and the garden is free of weeds. This time can be productive if I'm thinking about my writing and working through problems in my mind. But much of it isn't, and I have to get myself back to my desk.

Other people add rituals to their procrastination. The best description I know is in Wallace Markfield's *To an Early Grave*, which was made into a movie called *Bye-Bye, Braverman*. A writer is composing a review:

> Levine paced his den, his study, his writing chamber with slow steps. Then, by devious ways—tamping down the shavings in his pencil sharpener, giving a just-so twist to his gooseneck lamp, swabbing an ash tray, squirting the lightest of oils into his Olivetti and a few drops of Windex on the plate glass of his desk—he regained a measure of repose.

After doodling on his notes with blue and red pencils,

> from the lower left corner of his desk he took up a book of paper matches, he twisted off one match and, with utmost delicacy, leaving the head intact and no end frayed or split, peeled it into four parts, and each of these parts he peeled into four more parts.
> Then, then Levine judged himself ready.

Levine managed to write one paragraph before moving on to the next stage, in which he straightened out the refrigerator, cleaned the stove (including the oven), emptied and relined the garbage pail, and closely examined the *Playboy* centerfold. Then he went through the match routine again before squeezing out another sentence (pp. 80–84).

Now that you've read about Levine, you may be able to end this sort of time-wasting simply by recalling the image. If not, remove all temptations and try to laugh at yourself when you give in.

The best way to avoid writing problems is to become proficient enough that writing is no longer painful. Writing will always be difficult, but it need not be worse than cleaning the oven.

Working steadily, regularly, every day should clear up bad habits and, in a few months, make you a better, more comfortable writer.

Speaking of procrastination, it's time to stop reading and start writing. We've given you our very best advice, to which I will now add our collective best wishes for success.

FREQUENTLY ASKED QUESTIONS

How long is a book?
A book is as long as it needs to be to accomplish its task, and no longer. The subject and purpose should determine the length, and there is no arbitrary minimum or maximum. With that said, however, let us provide more concrete advice. A book can be anywhere from about 175 pages to several volumes. A book that began as a dissertation should fall toward the shorter end of that scale and should certainly run no more than one volume of 300 book pages, including notes and bibliography. This translates into about 400 to 500 double-spaced manuscript pages. That is the maximum. Shorter is better.

How long is a chapter?
A chapter should present a coherent story or argument. As a rule of thumb, chapters should be about 20 to 40 book pages long, exclusive of notes. That translates into 35 to 70 double-spaced manuscript pages. Don't worry too much about this, but watch out for

chapters that are much longer or much shorter than your other chapters (except for introductions and conclusions, which are often shorter). This kind of irregularity usually arises when one topic is covered too skimpily, when one chapter is too detailed, or when you have tried to combine in one chapter two or more topics that belong apart. Figure out what the problem is and revise accordingly.

How many notes should a book or chapter have?
As few as necessary to give credit where it is due. (See Chapter 5.) If you insist on numbers: *never* more than one per sentence, and preferably one per paragraph; *never* more than ninety-nine per chapter, and preferably many fewer.

Can I get the publisher to put my notes at the foot of the page?
Probably not. It is more difficult and time-consuming to print footnotes rather than endnotes. Only if there is a very good reason to do this are you likely to persuade your editor. (See Chapter 5.)

Is it all right to publish material from my dissertation in journals if I plan to include it in my book?
It is a good idea to publish an article or at least give a conference paper related to your dissertation because it may attract the attention of acquiring editors. However, you cannot publish very much of it. Most presses set the limit, formally or informally, at 20 to 25 percent. In most cases, the material should be revised from the journal version. (A journal article, after all, is freestanding; a book chapter is part of a larger work.) Always inform

prospective book publishers about what has been published elsewhere and how the two versions compare. Some publishers will ask you to complete a form that provides this information. Remember, too, that if you have transferred the copyright in an article to the journal, you may need permission to use it again. Check your contract with the journal. A common practice, and one that makes both journal and book publishers happy, is to publish material in a journal and then summarize that material with a citation to the more detailed article.

How long does it take to get a book published?
It takes anywhere from three months to more than a year to have a manuscript reviewed and accepted, and even longer if the first press rejects it. After it is accepted, you may need a few months to complete required revisions. Once the manuscript is ready to be edited and typeset, you should count on a minimum of nine months, and a year is more realistic. In other words, it will probably take two to three years from the time you submit your manuscript to the time you have bound books.

Should I ask scholars in my field to review the manuscript before submitting it?
Although it is a good idea to seek advice, you should not ask too many people to read the whole manuscript. It is a major imposition, and it takes a lot of your time as well as theirs. In addition, by reading it for you, these scholars may disqualify themselves as readers for a press. Nor will journal editors select people listed in the acknowledgments as reviewers. Seek help strategically: there are only so many experts, and you need to conserve them.

Should I copyright my dissertation?

Your dissertation is protected by copyright without your doing anything at all. If you wish to include a copyright notice, that is perfectly all right, but it is not necessary. There is no reason to register the dissertation with the copyright office. In fact, that will just make it slightly harder for the publisher to register it as a book.

How many illustrations can I include?

That depends on the nature of your manuscript and the importance of the illustrations. Publishers will welcome illustrations if they are essential to the argument of the book or if they will enhance its salability. They will not want to include them if they are peripheral or merely decorative. Remember, too, that the author is responsible for acquiring usable prints as well as permission to use artwork, whether photographs, drawings, or maps. This is a time-consuming and sometimes expensive task. (See Chapter 9.)

When should I start looking for a publisher?

As soon as you know what your book is about, can write a good prospectus, have an introduction and at least one revised chapter to send, and have a fair idea of when the book will be finished. If a publisher expresses interest earlier than that, promise to send them material as soon as possible but do not rush to send material that isn't ready for public viewing.

PLANNING TOOLS

To help you plan and schedule your work, I have provided a list and a chart. The list enumerates some short pieces of writing that you should prepare to help you focus your thoughts, present your work to potential publishers and granting agencies, and keep you on track as you revise and rewrite. The chart has three columns: years and semesters (summer, fall, spring); some possible tasks for that period (not inclusive or mandatory, but possible and advisable); and the tasks you schedule for that period (for you to fill in). You can use this chart to plan, to chart your progress, and to see whether you are falling behind. You can begin filling it in from either end.

WRITING TO HELP YOUR WRITING

A number of short writing exercises will help you prepare for the larger task of writing your book. Each item includes a description and a list of uses. These can be revised as your ideas become clearer and your work progresses. Keep these materials within view of your workplace.

1. *A one-sentence description of your book project.* This sentence will help you focus as you write and, once memorized, will provide a way to open e-mail and personal conversations with editors.

2. *A one-paragraph description of your book project.* Depending on how you write this, it may remind you of the structure you have chosen, the narrative path your book will take, or some other central feature of your work. It will provide the most important paragraph in your cover letter to editors and will be useful in the narrative of your grant applications.

3. *A list of things to be removed from the dissertation.* This will help guide your revisions.

4. *A list of articles that might be drawn from the things you will remove.* For example, the chapter on methodology might turn into a brief statement in your book but provide material for a journal article.

5. *A list of material to be added.* This will help guide your revisions and will help you plan and schedule further research and writing.

6. *A table of contents.* Once you have decided what to remove and add, compiling a table of contents should help you organize your ideas and give you a basis for planning. You can begin with a simple list of chapter titles and gradually expand it so that you have a paragraph-long description of each chapter.

7. *A description of your audience.* This may be generic ("all Shakespeare scholars"), specific (economists, political scientists, and historians interested in Latin America), or personal (educated general readers like Aunt Mildred and Uncle Henry).

8. *A list of grant possibilities.* These may range from full-year fellowships to small travel grants; the sources may range from
   national and international foundations to government agencies to your own institution. Be sure to include deadlines for
   applications.

9. *A list of possible illustrations, if appropriate.* This will give you
   an early start on what can be a time-consuming task.

10. *A list of possible titles.* This may provide inspiration and,
    though none may be used, it's fun to do.

PLANNING YOUR WORK

Summer 20

POSSIBLE PROJECTS	YOUR PROJECTS
Apply for grants	
Work on article unrelated to book	

Fall 20

POSSIBLE PROJECTS	YOUR PROJECTS
Re-read and focus manuscript	
Plan further research	
Order research materials	
Plan articles	
Think about revision	

*Spring 20*_____

POSSIBLE PROJECTS	YOUR PROJECTS
Begin further research	
Work on paper or article	
Think about revision	

*Summer 20*_____

POSSIBLE PROJECTS	YOUR PROJECTS
Apply for grants	
Continue research	
Write paper or article	
Begin manuscript revisions	

*Fall 20*_____

POSSIBLE PROJECTS	YOUR PROJECTS
Submit article	
Continue manuscript revisions	
Plan next paper or article	

*Spring 20*_____

POSSIBLE PROJECTS   YOUR PROJECTS

Present paper
Continue manuscript revisions

_____

_____

_____

_____

_____

_____

*Summer 20*_____

POSSIBLE PROJECTS   YOUR PROJECTS

Continue manuscript revisions
Prepare book prospectus
Apply for grants

_____

_____

_____

_____

_____

*Fall 20*_____

POSSIBLE PROJECTS   YOUR PROJECTS

Submit book prospectus
Write paper or article
Begin writing book

_____

_____

_____

_____

_____

Spring 20

POSSIBLE PROJECTS

Present paper
Find publisher
Write book

YOUR PROJECTS

_____
_____
_____
_____
_____
_____

Summer 20

POSSIBLE PROJECTS

Finish book
Submit manuscript to publisher
Write grant proposal

YOUR PROJECTS

_____
_____
_____
_____
_____
_____

Fall 20

POSSIBLE PROJECTS

Work on paper or article
Think about new project

YOUR PROJECTS

_____
_____
_____
_____
_____
_____

Spring 20

POSSIBLE PROJECTS   YOUR PROJECTS

Respond to reviewers

Revise book manuscript

Summer 20

POSSIBLE PROJECTS   YOUR PROJECTS

Complete manuscript revisions

Work on paper or article

Write grant proposal

Fall 20

POSSIBLE PROJECTS   YOUR PROJECTS

Work on paper or article

Review copyediting

Spring/Summer 20

POSSIBLE PROJECTS   YOUR PROJECTS
Work on other projects
Proofread book galleys
Prepare book index

Summer 20

POSSIBLE PROJECTS   YOUR PROJECTS
Write sabbatical proposal
Focus on next project

USEFUL READING

FINDING A PUBLISHER

Derricourt, Robin M. *An Author's Guide to Scholarly Publishing.* Princeton: Princeton University Press, 1996.

This epistolary handbook covers the basics of preparing a manuscript, writing a proposal, understanding a publisher's response, dealing with production and marketing, and understanding the role of publishing in academe.

Germano, William P. *Getting It Published: A Guide for Scholars and Anyone Else Serious about Serious Books.* Chicago: University of Chicago Press, 2001.

In the shortest of the guides, Germano covers the choice of publisher, proposal writing, contracts, permissions, and production.

Harman, Eleanor, Ian Montagnes, Siobhan McMenemy, and Chris Bucci, eds. *The Thesis and the Book: A Guide for First-Time Academic Authors.* Toronto: University of Toronto Press, 2003.

A revised and expanded edition of a classic, based on articles that originally appeared in *Scholarly Publishing.*

Luey, Beth. *Handbook for Academic Authors*. 4th ed. New York: Cambridge University Press, 2002.

Luey offers advice on writing and publishing journal articles; finding and working with scholarly publishers, textbook publishers, and trade houses; manuscript preparation; and permissions. She includes chapters on electronic publishing and on the economics of scholarly publishing, as well as an annotated bibliography.

Rabiner, Susan, and Alfred Fortunato. *Thinking Like Your Editor: How to Write Great Serious Nonfiction — And Get It Published*. New York: Norton, 2002.

This book is directed at authors preparing trade books for general readers, but it is full of good ideas and information for any nonfiction writer.

WRITING AND PLANNING

Hancock, Elise. *Ideas into Words: Mastering the Craft of Science Writing*. Baltimore: Johns Hopkins University Press, 2003.

The author is a science writer, and her advice is geared to journalists writing about science for general readers. The book will nevertheless be helpful to scientists who wish to make their work understandable to a lay audience.

Horton, Susan R. *Thinking through Writing*. Baltimore: Johns Hopkins University Press, 1982.

This basic manual focuses on the purpose and process of writing rather than on the nuts and bolts.

Rankin, Elizabeth. *The Work of Writing: Insights and Strategies for Academics and Professionals*. San Francisco: Jossey-Bass, 2001.

The advice in this book focuses on audience and voice, and the author guides writers through thinking and decision making.

Strunk, W., Jr., and E. B. White. *The Elements of Style*. 4th ed. Boston: Allyn & Bacon, 2000.

This is the only grammar book you'll ever need. It provides clear, concise, and memorable advice on grammar, punctuation, and usage, emphasizing the need for brevity and clarity.

Zerubavel, Eviatar. *The Clockwork Muse: A Practical Guide to Writing Theses, Dissertations, and Books.* Cambridge: Harvard University Press, 1999.
The author provides advice on setting up a schedule, planning your writing, and establishing good writing habits. The advice helps with revision as well as writing.

ABOUT THE CONTRIBUTORS

JENNIFER CREWE is editorial director at Columbia University Press. She has acquired books in various fields in the humanities for twenty years, for Columbia and for Macmillan Inc. and Charles Scribners Sons. She has an M.F.A. in writing from Columbia University.

PETER J. DOUGHERTY is group publisher for the social sciences and senior economics editor of Princeton University Press. His book *Who's Afraid of Adam Smith?* was published by John Wiley & Sons in 2002. His articles on publishing have appeared in the *Journal of Scholarly Publishing*, the *Journal of Economic Literature*, and the *Chronicle of Higher Education*.

TREVOR LIPSCOMBE is the editor in chief of the Johns Hopkins University Press and sits on the advisory board of the *Journal of Scholarly Publishing*. He has a doctorate in theoretical physics from Oxford University and has published research and pedagogical articles in both physics and mathematics. Prior to Hopkins, he was a member of the editorial staff of the journal *Physical Review* and then an acquisitions editor for Princeton University Press.

BETH LUEY is the founding director of the Scholarly Publishing Program at Arizona State University and the author of *Handbook for Academic*

Authors. She has been the editor of *Publishing Research Quarterly* and *Documentary Editing.*

JUDY METRO is editor in chief at the National Gallery of Art, Washington, D.C., and was for many years senior editor and manager of the art book workshop at Yale University Press. From 1985 to 2000 she was a critic in graphic design at the Yale School of Art.

CHARLES T. MYERS is editor for political science, law, and classics at Princeton University Press. Previously he served as editor for political science and law at the University of Michigan Press. He earned a Ph.D. in political science from the University of Michigan.

SCOTT NORTON worked in corporate and legal publishing before entering academic publishing as a freelance editor in 1993. Since 1995, he has served in various editorial roles on the staff of the University of California Press, where he is currently a developmental editor and project manager for science.

ANN REGAN is managing editor at the Minnesota Historical Society Press and Borealis Books.

WILLIAM P. SISLER began his publishing career in 1973 as humanities editor at the Johns Hopkins University Press. In 1983 he joined Oxford University Press (USA) as executive editor for the humanities and social sciences and was named a vice-president in 1987. He was appointed director of Harvard University Press in 1990.

SANFORD G. THATCHER was an editor at Princeton University Press for twenty-two years before becoming director of Penn State University Press in 1989. He served as president of the Association of American University Presses in 2007–2008.

JOHANNA E. VONDELING received her Ph.D. in English from the University of Texas at Austin. She has worked for W. W. Norton and Holt, Rinehart and Winston and was until recently an acquisitions editor for Jossey-Bass Publishers in San Francisco.

JENYA WEINERB is the managing editor at Yale University Press.

INDEX

accessibility, and audience, 138
advance, on royalties, 197–98
advice: from colleagues, 156–57,
163, 243; from editors, 206; in
graduate school, 8, 20; importance of, 11; from readers outside field, 138–39
American Historical Association,
on tenure requirements, 39
anecdotes, 22, 140
aphorism, 82
appendix, use of, 23, 143
archival journals, 168, 169
articles. *See* journal articles
attribution, 83. *See also* documentation
audience: for art books, 186; and
documentation, 105–6, 125–27;
expansion of, 137–38, 153–55;
expectations of, 17–18, 19, 133,
209, 217–18; and format,
226–27; identification of, 18–19,
43–44, 73, 222–23; and illustra-

tions, 190–91; and price, 141;
for professional books, 213–16;
and revision, 73; and style, 138;
and topic, 24–25
author-date references system,
115–18

bibliographic essay, 114–15
bibliography: annotated, 115; need
for, 113; organization of, 114;
reduction of, 23, 113, 143
biography: as book genre, 26–28,
92; quotation in, 99
books: length of, 67, 141–42, 155,
241; in science, 170–71

camera copy, of illustrations,
187–88
chapters: length of, 45, 62, 241–42;
opening of, 140; structure of,
63–64; thesis statements for,
61–62; titles of, 22–23, 45–46,
92–93

COMPOSITOR:	Binghamton Valley Composition, LLC
TEXT:	10/15 Janson
DISPLAY:	DINSchriften
PRINTER AND BINDER:	Maple-Vail Manufacturing Group